D1216620

This

... is an authorized facsimile made from the master copy of the original book. Further unauthorized copying is prohibited.

Books on Demand is a publishing service of UMI. The program offers xerographic reprints of more than 136,000 books that are no longer in print.

The primary focus of Books on Demand is academic and professional resource materials originally published by university presses, academic societies, and trade book publishers worldwide.

UMI
BOOKS ON DEMAND™

UMI
A Bell & Howell Company
300 North Zeeb Road ❧ PO Box 1346
Ann Arbor, Michigan 48106-1346
800-521-0600 ❧ 313-761-4700

Printed in 1997 by xerographic process on acid-free paper

Schizophrenia

The Experience and Its Treatment

Werner M. Mendel

With Contributions by Robert E. Allen

Foreword by R. Bruce Sloane

Schizophrenia

The Experience and Its Treatment

Jossey-Bass Publishers

San Francisco • London • 1986

616.8982
M5238
1976

SCHIZOPHRENIA
The Experience and Its Treatment
by Werner M. Mendel

Copyright © 1976 by: Jossey-Bass, Inc., Publishers
433 California Street
San Francisco, California 94104
&
Jossey-Bass Limited
28 Banner Street
London EC1Y 8QE

Library of Congress Catalogue Card Number LC 76-20083

International Standard Book Number ISBN 0-87589-296-5

Manufactured in the United States of America

JACKET DESIGN BY WILLI BAUM
FIRST EDITION
    First printing: September 1976
    Second printing: October 1979
    Third printing: October 1981
    Fourth printing: January 1986

Code 7611

❧❧❧❧❧❧❧❧

The Jossey-Bass
Behavioral Science Series

Foreword

Although Werner Mendel has often talked to me of schizophrenia, it was not until I read this book that I realized both his voluminous grasp of the subject and his dedication. Not many psychiatrists in this field retain both an appetitive drive for discovery and the staying power through the long haul of the illness. For an illness it surely is, whatever the controversies of its cause.

A simple classification of psychiatry is to divide it into minor and major. The "little problems of living" assumed by some to be justification for the concern of the psychiatrist wane in the light of the overwhelming problems of living suffered by those suffering from schizophrenia. Some years ago Mendel was criticized, as a psycho-analyst, for diverting his writing, studies, and practice to the narcis-sistic neuroses, such as schizophrenia, which responded poorly to psychoanalysis. The answer to such criticism might justifiably have been because schizophrenia is *important*. Those of us who believe that the "little problems of living" and the neuroses wax and wane perhaps almost regardless of their treatment, could never say the same about schizophrenia. Here there is no panacea. If psycho-therapy always worked, it would clearly be the treatment of choice; but sometimes it does, and sometimes it does not. If psychotropic medication always proved successful, there would be no need to look for other remedies. Unfortunately, despite the major improve-ments medication has wrought, some patients do not respond. The enigma of schizophrenia might well occupy a young psychiatrist rather than the trivia that so often befuddle his or her mind. Schizophrenia would give the therapist something to bite on, but not many have jaws that are strong enough.

What is schizophrenia? This question, which has been bandied about between the charlatans and the scientists, is answered in this volume. A life-style it may be, but it is not *only* a life-style. Diagnosticians, like golfers, gardeners, and fishermen, fall into the lumpers and the splitters. A European psychiatrist of my acquaint-ance said a friend of his never diagnosed schizophrenia in anybody he liked, because schizophrenia was universally incurable. To some American psychiatrists the world trembles with schizophrenia, which they find around every corner. Somewhere in the middle must lie the truth and this volume seeks to tease it out.

How should schizophrenia be treated? The author leans heavily to lifetime support. There are few who would cavil. Schizo-phrenia is not a benign condition. With the best aftercare in the world, more than 40 percent of sufferers fail to achieve even a social remission five years after its onset. For this reason, the treatment regime here advocated is holistic and flexible. Too often the "pill doctors" have sneered at the "talk doctors" and vice versa. Werner Mendel skillfully blends all approaches. Above all, his skill and ex-perience in the psychopathology of the illness shows through. Until we make some biological or other breakthrough, and quite possibly even then, we will need therapists who are knowledgable in the psychology of the disease. This book will point the way.

R. Bruce Sloane, M.D.,
Chairman and Professor, Department of Psychiatry,
University of Southern California School of Medicine

To LORI

The circle of existential time!

⧓⧓⧓⧓⧓⧓⧓

Preface

Many patterns of disorganized behavior have been labeled as illnesses but have not been clearly related to demonstrable biological errors or tissue pathologies. Among such illnesses is schizophrenia. In this book I define schizophrenia as a chronic illness with a number of disabilities, a known natural history, and a response to treatment and nontreatment in a predictable way. The observations, speculations, and conclusions I present are based on longitudinal observations of human beings with disabilities and difficulties that are generally called schizophrenia. It has become quite clear to me that cross-sectional studies of large numbers of patients do not give

an adequate picture of schizophrenia and, in fact, frequently lead
to erroneous diagnoses. Only by following individual patients for
many years can we begin to understand what schizophrenia is,
what it does to human lives, and how it is different from other
mental illnesses. It is crucial that we recognize that the disabilities
of schizophrenia are imbedded in the total life situations of individuals. These disabilities consist of *failure of effective anxiety
management, failure of interpersonal relationships,* and *failure of
historicity.*

  Schizophrenia: The Experience and Its Treatment is a short
book. Yet by this brevity I hope to convey that, although there is
much speculation, very little is known about schizophrenia. My
purpose is to present an overview of schizophrenia and describe a
group of people whose lives are impaired by this illness. The first
section on phenomenology offers a theory and technique of observation and a description of schizophrenia. The second section on
etiology—which is particularly brief, since almost nothing is known
with certainty about the cause of this illness—summarizes the
present scope of speculation. The third section presents a rational
approach to therapy and discusses my twenty-five years of experience in treating individuals who have lived their lives with
schizophrenia.

  This work is intended for both specialists and students in the
mental health field. To the experienced clinician I offer new tools
for studying and observing patients, as well as a practical approach
to treatment. To the novice clinician and student I offer a system of
observing individual human beings who are afflicted with schizophrenia and a basis for understanding something about the pattern
of disorganized existence found in this illness. To the science of
human behavior I offer a theory of schizophrenia based on longitudinal phenomenological observations of hundreds of patients over a
quarter of a century and a method of treatment based on that
theory.

Los Angeles, California   Werner M. Mendel
July 1976

Contents

Part II.   Theories of Etiology

Part III.   Treatment Interventions

❧❧❧❧❧❧❧❧❧

Schizophrenia

The Experience and Its Treatment

Introduction

❧❧❧❧❧❧❧❧

The Problem of Schizophrenia

This book is about people whose lives are impaired by a cluster of disabilities. This impairment has been called an *illness*, a *life-style*, a *defect*, or an *existential foundering*. Whatever one chooses to call these problems in living, however one chooses to look at these difficulties, whatever theoretical orientation one brings to the task of observation, there is ample and firm evidence that the condition schizophrenia exists. Since earliest recorded history, there have been descriptions of human beings whose behavior, thinking, and feeling have been recognized as different, abnormal, sick, or possessed. This deviant behavior has fallen into three major categories: the depressions, the manias, and those disorders that we now

1

call *schizophrenia*. It is with this last category of deviancy that we are concerned.

A book on the topic of schizophrenia written in the 1970s is necessarily a book of clinical observation and of speculation. The only data we have are the observed behavior of people who experience the difficulty we call *schizophrenia*. This verbal and nonverbal behavior, which includes self-reporting by the patients, gives us a rich base of observation to begin our attempt at understanding this condition. Our observation of biochemistry, neurophysiology, and other biological factors adds to that base. Understanding the human being who has schizophrenic difficulties in his or her interaction with others individually and in groups gives us further observations and data. Experimental interventions of a chemical, psychological, and social nature that we call *treatment* give us additional data to broaden our base of understanding.

Yet any book on the topic of schizophrenia written in the 1970s must contain a clear statement that differentiates between observation and inference, between knowledge and speculation. Too frequently during the past fifty years, readers of books on this topic have been confused precisely because speculations were presented as fact, because questions were presented as answers, and because useful inferences were confused with observations.

I must say, before you begin reading this material based on my observations of schizophrenic existences over the past twenty years, that I do not know what causes schizophrenia. I do not know how to prevent schizophrenia, and I do not know how to cure schizophrenia. Yet the years that I have spent observing people who have the cluster of disorders in living that generally fall within the limits of what we choose to call *schizophrenia* have taught me much that I can share with you about this condition. I know how to recognize it, how to differentiate it from other conditions, how to differentiate one human being who has this difficulty from another who has the same difficulty. I know how to intervene helpfully in the lives of schizophrenic patients and I know how to prevent complications. I can help the person afflicted by schizophrenia to maximize his functioning in spite of his schizophrenic condition. In many ways, I am in exactly the same position as I am in regard to a number of illnesses that have been known to medicine for some time. For example, we do not know what causes diabetes, we do not know how to prevent it, and we do not know how to cure it. We know a lot about some of the intervening etiological variables such as sugar metabolism, fat metabolism, and insulin production and secretion. We have some experience in treatment to prevent complications, to minimize disabilities, to maximize function, and to prevent death. We can say exactly the same about our diagnostic and treatment skills regarding schizophrenia.

The observations, speculations, and conclusions presented in this book are based on the longitudinal observation of human beings who have the disabilities and difficulties that are generally called *schizophrenia*. It has become quite clear to us that cross-sectional studies of large numbers of patients do not give an adequate picture of schizophrenia and in fact frequently lead to erroneous diagnosis. Only by following patients for fifteen or twenty years, as we have done, can we begin to understand what schizophrenia is, what it does to human lives, and how it is different from other mental illnesses.

Diagnostic fashions change from time to time and place to place. In the 1950s, for example, when we started working, the schizophrenias were called *schizophrenic reactions*. This phrase implied a set of attitudes toward the illness that are quite different from attitudes implied now that we call it *schizophrenia*.

One of the outcomes of the longitudinal approach to understanding human beings who have schizophrenia is to recognize that such diagnostic labels are frequently determined by the individual, the organization, or the place where the label is applied. Often these labels have little relationship to what is going on in the patient. When we started working, many patients were diagnosed as *catatonic schizophrenics*. Today, this diagnosis is relatively rare and the label of *chronic undifferentiated schizophrenia* is much more common. The term *paranoid schizophrenics* represents a more frequent diagnosis in some of the European countries than in the United States. With the recent renewed interest in the affective illnesses, the diagnosis of *schizoaffective schizophrenia* has again become more popular. Thus the fashions change and the labels change. Even our understanding of *process schizophrenia* versus *reactive schizophrenia* changes. But what does not change is the disability, the discomfort, and the chaos of human lives marred by schizophrenia.

Although we know little about the topic of schizophrenia, we do know a lot more than we use. The 1976 approach to the diagnosis and treatment of schizophrenia tends to be fragmented, swayed by fashions, and directed by the current theory. When we look at these fashions and theories, we discover that they tend to focus on some small aspect of the total problem and frequently supply only new vocabulary for old knowledge. Many recent studies of schizophrenia also tend to focus on signs and symptoms that are secondary or tertiary outcomes of the difficulties in living that the schizophrenic person experiences. Our approach is to recognize the known causal sequences between disability and symptom formation. By thus separating disability and symptom we can define the basic cluster of disabilities that result in the clinical picture called *schizophrenia*. We correlate clinical observation and practical treatment approaches with a logically rational theory of illness and treatment. We do not avoid speculation, but we clearly differentiate observation from speculation.

Chapter 1

※※※※※※※※

Changing Patterns of Description

The scientific method is based on detailed and carefully recorded observation of behavior. These observations are organized into a data base that becomes the foundation for the development of inferences. The inferences are the beginning of a theory leading to the classification of observations. Such a theory then points the way to more concise and more reliable observations leading to the further refinement of the theory. In this process, it is of the utmost importance that the observations be clearly differentiated from inferences.

In the field of psychiatry, the data consist entirely of the observation of verbal and nonverbal human behavior. Unfortu-

5

nately, the tendency to confuse inferences with observation is seen
not only in the beginning student but even in some senior members
of research teams. There is a tendency to reify concepts to an extent
that useful scientific fictions based on inferences are treated as
though they were facts derived from direct observation. For example, anxiety and depression are not observations. They are inferences, though indeed low-level inferences. What I observe is an
individual who is unable to sit still, who has sweaty palms when I
shake his hand, and who reports that he* feels uneasy and fidgety.
From this behavior, I infer that the individual is anxious. I do not
observe his anxiety. I am probably quite correct in my inference,
although in fact I may be totally mistaken. The subject may be
suffering from a fever and may mislabel his subjective self-reporting
of uneasiness and dread, because of his own misinterpretation of a
febrile state, as anxiety. When I make higher-level inferences, about
ego states or superego lacunae, for example, then indeed I am
venturing far afield. These high-level inferences based on a theory
must always be identified as such and must not be confused with
observation. We do not have ego scopes or id retractors or superego
calibrators; our inferences are based on nonexistent observations.
Such inferences are useful scientific fictions that allow the profes-
sionals to talk to each other and to describe to each other certain
clusters of function. These useful scientific fictions are of value only
when those who use them understand the underlying theoretical
assumptions and can clearly recognize the difference between a
scientific fiction and an observation. However, in no way is this
qualification meant to discredit scientific fictions.

In physics, the volt is a scientific fiction used to describe the
difference in potential between two electrical points, but the volt
does not in fact exist. Similarly, in the description of human behavior, ego functions do not exist, since ego does not exist. Rather, the
concept of ego is a way for us to describe adaptive capacities of
the individual and to communicate with each other about these

---

* The traditional use of the pronoun *he* has not yet been superseded
by a convenient, generally accepted pronoun that means either *he* or *she*.
Therefore, the author will continue to use *he*, and hereby takes the opportunity to acknowledge the inherent inequity of the traditional preference for
the masculine pronoun.

capacities, using a shorthand language that can be understood by all who subscribe to the psychoanalytic theory of human behavior.

Once we have made it quite clear that we must at all times strive for precise differentiation between inferences and observation, we can then look at the changing patterns of observation and description. In the latter part of the nineteenth century, the German professors of psychiatry were masters of descriptive techniques. Their descriptions consisted of detailed observations of behavior. They looked at an individual's behavior much as one would look at a slide under the microscope. Their descriptions convey a picture of a patient that comes alive on the pages of a textbook even a century later. Emil Kraepelin, at the University of Munich, wrote:

> Gentlemen, the patient you see before you today is a merchant, 43 years old, who has been in our hospital almost uninterruptedly for about five years. He is strongly built, but badly nourished, and has a pale complexion, and an invalid expression of face. He comes in with short, weary steps, sits down slowly, and remains sitting in a rather bent position, staring in front of him almost without moving. When questioned, he turns his head a little, and, after a certain pause, answers softly, and in monosyllables, but to the point. We get the impression that speaking gives him a great deal of trouble, his lips moving for a little while before the sound comes out. The patient is clear about time and place, knows the doctors, and says that he has been ill for more than five years, but cannot give any further explanation of this than that his spirits are affected. He says he has no apprehension. He gives short and perfectly relevant answers to questions about his circumstances and past life. He does exercises and arithmetic slowly but correctly, even when they are fairly difficult. He writes his name on the blackboard, when asked to do so, with firm though hesitating strokes, after having got up awkwardly [1904, p. 11].

Another description from the same period is by Emil Mendel, professor of psychiatry at the University of Berlin. He describes a case of "acute dementia" in the following words: "The patient knows neither his age nor dwelling, scarcely his name. Sometimes he does not answer at all, and scarcely shows any mental activity. With this his gaze is directed to a distance, his mouth is half open, the saliva trickles therefrom, the lines of his countenance are lax and betray no expression. The patient must be fed, he passes urine and feces involuntarily. The pulse is generally retarded, the temperature subnormal" (1907, p. 65)'.

At the beginning of the twentieth century, primarily through the ingenious contributions of Sigmund Freud, a new emphasis was placed on the observation and collection of the patient's self-reported accounts of his feelings and thoughts. Freud, in scrupulous and meticulous detail, recorded all of the things that patients said, using as his basic data this self-reporting of the patient's thoughts, feelings, dreams, and experiences. The subjective reality of the individual became the primary data base. In the modern writings on schizophrenia by researchers such as Ludwig Binswanger, Otto Will, and Frieda Fromm-Reichman, as well as in our own work, a great deal of material has been collected demonstrating the pain and agony, the emptiness and alienation that patients convey when they describe their own world of schizophrenia. Following are some examples:

> 1. "I am like a zombie living behind a glass wall. I can see all that goes on in the world but I can't touch it. I can't reach it. I can't be in contact with it. I am outside. They are inside and when I get inside, they aren't there. There is nothing there, absolutely nothing."

> 2. "Nothing is me. Nothing is mine. I don't live in my body. I don't live anywhere. My body just is. It is like the strings are being pulled and it is moved automatically. But I haven't anything in it."

> 3. "I have experienced this process chiefly as a condition in which the integrating mental picture in my personality was taken away and smashed to bits, leaving me like agitated hamburger distributed infinitely throughout the universe."

Such self-reporting adds much to the data base beyond the external description of behavior given by Kraepelin and Emil Mendel. However, neither the collection of self-reported verbalizations nor the descriptions from the outside of the patient's verbal and nonverbal behavior are complete in themselves. Each extends our data base, each tells us more about the states of illness. Yet these two approaches to the observation of behavior alone do not give us as complete a picture as we can have with further extension of observations.

Ever since the development of instruments in the psychology laboratories to measure physiological functions that are altered by emotional states, we have had the ability to measure and observe various tissue behavior, thus further expanding our data base. This expansion includes such measurements as blood pressure, pulse rate, skin temperature, psychogalvanic skin responses, extraocular movements, changes in penis volume, and changes in blood flow. These physiological recordings can be correlated with the observation of behavior and with the subjective self-reporting by the patient. Then more valid inferences lead to more useful classifications and more productive theories of human behavior in illness and in health.

To complete the observations available to us, we must recognize that man lives in an environment and that his behavior is determined by his interaction with that environment. We recognize that as we interact with an individual for purposes of observing his behavior we are in fact intervening in that behavior. The interaction includes the culture, role expectancy, and other aspects of the perceived environment. An example of the influence of the observer on the data he collects is in the choice of metaphor that is dictated by the roles of patient and physician. In my role as a psychiatrist, role expectancy leads my patients to behave in such a way that they talk to me about their feelings, their thoughts, their dreams, and their interpersonal relationships. They will tell me that they are anxious and frightened, that they are feeling blue, or that their thoughts are blocked. If I were a dermatologist, the same patient would come to me with these same problems, only the metaphor would be the skin and he would talk to me about his itching and redness, he would complain that he cannot sleep because he has creepy-crawly feelings, and that he cannot go out in public or meet

people because they are repelled by his acne. If I were a gastroen-
terologist, the same patient would talk to me about the discomfort
and gas he has after eating, and the special diets he has tried, and
how his gastrointestinal problems interfere with his social life because
he cannot tolerate many foods and must be careful to eat only what
has been especially prepared for him. The metaphor, which is the
patient's entrance ticket to the helping situation, is dictated not only
by the patient's primary symptoms but to a large extent by the label
I wear as a representative of the helping situation. In this way we
helpers alter observable behavior.

Once the observations have been made and the data have
been collected, we are ready to make certain inferences leading to
classifications and eventually diagnostic categories. In recent years,
there has been an antidiagnostic prejudice among our younger
colleagues in psychiatry. This prejudice has been based on their
observations that diagnostic categories lack reliability and that con-
sequently diagnostic labels have been misused. Both of these criti-
cisms are entirely justified. Diagnosis has been based too long on
local prejudices and geographic fashions rather than on careful
observation and collection of data. The problem of diagnostic
unreliability has been the subject of extensive research in an attempt
to find a uniformly acceptable system of reliable diagnostic classifications for mental illness. At the present time agreement about
diagnostic categories has increased somewhat in various parts of the
world, although differences still remain. Diagnoses have been used
as labels and have tended to interfere with the understanding of
the individual patient, his problem, his treatment, and his position
in society. However, the difficulty and misuse of diagnosis do not
invalidate its proper use. As long as we remember that diagnoses
are only generalizations, and that one schizophrenic patient is
different from another schizophrenic patient, just as one psychiatric
resident physician is different from another psychiatric resident
physician, the "diagnostic categories" can serve us well. Diagnosis
defines brackets of pathology, states prognostic expectancy, and
outlines a treatment approach.

When we make the inference that a certain cluster of observed disabilities and defects in functions represent a disease
category, then we are also making assumptions about what is

normal and what is abnormal. Inferences about normality are useful as long as those who use the concepts understand the theoretical basis from which their decision arises. There are a variety of ways in which normality is decided in human behavior. Normality is not absolute, nor are the concepts on which ideas of normality are based clearly defined.

Let us begin looking at this problem by reminding ourselves that the Latin word *norma* means "ruler," which was the rod used to measure. When we use the word *normal*, we are referring to a measure. In medicine, and therefore in psychiatry, there are many approaches to the concept of normality.

The first and most frequent definition of the concept is a statistical one, in which we call *normal* that behavior that falls in the center of a normal distribution curve on an observed population. The terms *average, median,* and *within two standard deviations* are all means of describing observed behavior. What the concept of normality tells us is that if we observe ninety-eight people standing on their feet and two people standing on their heads, for this population of one hundred it is normal to stand on their feet and it is abnormal to stand on their heads. The statistical approach to the concept of normality may or may not be useful in understanding the individual patient and his problems. Self-definition is another concept of normality; the individual describes himself as normal or abnormal, depending on how he feels about himself. Another definition of normality and disease is the classification of discomfort and pain as always abnormal, and the absence of discomfort and pain as normal. Other definitions state that normal is to be functional and to be abnormal is to be dysfunctional. If something works, then it is normal; if it does not work, it is abnormal. Normality may also be autocratically determined by an outside authority who defines expected behavior as normal and any deviancy from the expectation as abnormal. On occasion, the observer and classifier of behavior will use himself as a standard of normality and will measure his observations of the behavior of others against that standard.

Each of these approaches to the concept of normality has serious limitations, but each also has some usefulness if we are precise in our definition, as well as aware of how the concept influences the specific observations and judgments we make.

The behavior that we observe, describe, categorize, and ultimately classify is the final common path of a multitude of influences. This path is not only the direct result of psychopathology. No matter how sick a patient is, no matter how dysfunctional and disorganized, he is more than only sick. Parts of him are well and part of his behavior is determined by many other aspects of being human. It is important that we constantly remind ourselves of this fact in understanding behavior. The behavior that I observe, including the verbal and nonverbal behavior, including any physiological measures and the self-reporting as well as the social interactions between the observer and the observed, is the result of what is right about the patient as well as what is wrong with him. The observed behavior is the result of the patient's culture, of his role at the moment, of his agenda in the interaction, of the expectancy I have for his behavior, and of his entire history, including all he has learned, all that has happened to him, and all of the genetic predispositions he has received. It is also the result of his physiological state and his biological background, of his anticipation of future events and his memory of the past. All of these factors come together in observable human behavior.

It is useful to classify the observations under certain headings. Each patient deserves a *personality description* or diagnosis in which we attempt to summarize the observations characteristic for the patient when he is not ill, characteristic of him as a person. How does he usually manage anxiety? How does he usually behave? What is his present observed behavior? What is his lifelong pattern of personality? We also need to describe, classify, and diagnostically summarize his *biological state*. We need to discuss the condition of his tissues and his general health. Then we need to describe the *social and cultural determinants* of the patient's behavior. Particularly when the observer is of a different social class or a different culture or ethnic group from the one being observed, he may tend to misinterpret such difference as psychopathology. Middle-class psychiatrists are particularly prone to call lower-class normal behavior *psychopathology* and to attempt to treat such behavior with medication or psychotherapy. If we remind ourselves to be aware of the contribution that social class and culture and ethnic background make to behavior, we can avoid such silly and potentially harmful mistakes. Finally, we need to describe the behavior that is related to the illness and that is the result of *psychopathology*. This last category of classification of behavior is the major topic of this book.

In order to understand the wide range of response offered by our society to individuals with aberrant behavior, it is necessary to go back into the remnants of prescientific thinking about behavior that persist. Demonology, criminality, and social learning approaches are still important aspects of modern society's response to abnormal human behavior. For example, the person who protests against the injustices of city government by walking down Main Street without clothing may be handled in a variety of ways in our society. How he is handled is determined in part by the accident of who comes on the scene to manage this behavior. If the man is arrested by the police, taken to jail, booked, charged with lewd conduct, and then brought before the judge, the whole transaction might be legal. He would be defined as a criminal having broken the law. His restitution would be a fine or a jail sentence, and the entire matter might be handled within the legal system. If this same act occurs in a lower-class ghetto and the intervention is made not by the police but by a social worker, the protest may be seen as justified and determined by the person's class status. The social worker may define the individual as a disenfranchised minority citizen, the act as a social protest and social disobedience. Restitution might be made by changing social conditions and in educating the protester to a more acceptable middle-class way of expressing his displeasure with city government. If the individual who is engaged in this behavior is a member of a religious community, the intervention might be made by a cleric who would define the act as a sin. The sinner would make restitution by repentance and prayer in terms of a theological system. Finally, if this act occurs in a community that has a certain psychiatric sophistication, the individual might be brought by the well-trained local police to a psychiatric emergency center where he would be diagnosed as mentally ill and defined as a patient. The transaction would be medical. The patient would be given medication and psychotherapy would be offered.

How we observe behavior, classify it, and respond to it is highly variable. Within the framework of the medical model, the clear differentiation between observations and inferences is a useful and necessary discipline that increases the reliability and replicability of our classification of observed behavior. Description from the outside, description from the inside, and transactional descriptions by participant observers provide the data from which inferences are developed.

In the study of schizophrenia, we begin with the data base of detailed and carefully recorded observations of behavior. These observations are classified into categories of signs and symptoms and become the basis for the predictable pattern of schizophrenia.

Chapter 2

☙☙☙☙☙☙☙☙

Classification of Signs and Symptoms

Physicians have attempted to make sense out of their observations of symptoms since the beginning of modern medicine. A number of symptoms have evolved that are based on theories of illness or theories of dysfunction. These systems view certain processes as primary or underlying, with other processes described as secondary or surface. Collections of signs and symptoms are related and classified to make up patterns of illness. Such a classification of signs and symptoms is usually tied to the theoretical bias of the observer. If he postulates an underlying organic process, he will speculate that only those symptoms related to such a postulated underlying process are primary, while all other symptoms are viewed as secondary.

An example of this approach is observed in Eugen Bleuler's classification of symptoms of schizophrenia. Bleuler (1950) called symptoms *primary* if they were related to a possible diffusely organic process. These primary symptoms of schizophrenia include thought process disorder, the somatic symptoms and the *Benommenheit* (stunnedness). Bleuler thought of all other symptoms as secondary, meaning that they were psychogenic reactions to the primary symptoms based on the postulated organicity. Others have designated the "dementia" as primary in schizophrenia. Emil Kraepelin (1904) saw all other symptoms of schizophrenia as secondary to the mental deterioration. The American psychiatrist Harry Stack Sullivan (1962) felt that the primary difficulty in schizophrenia was the impaired self-esteem and that everything else occuring in the schizophrenic symptom array could be understood as an attempt to repair this difficulty.

The students of Eugen Bleuler focused on the four fundamental symptoms of schizophrenia. These symptoms are not primary, in that they are not related to the postulated diffusely organic process. Rather, they are fundamental in that they are considered to be present in every case of schizophrenia. These four fundamental symptoms include the disturbances of association, affective indifference and inappropriateness, autism, and ambivalence. For the past fifty years many psychiatrists felt that all other symptoms of schizophrenia were accessory and could be explained as being caused by the fundamental symptoms. The son of Eugen Bleuler, Manfred Bleuler (1974) today believes that the basic essential, fundamental, primary problem in schizophrenia is autism. He thinks of all other signs and symptoms in schizophrenia as secondary to this problem. He coined the word *ambitendency* to replace *ambivalence,* noting that the patient is particularly bothered by his tendency to be immobilized by the equal motivation to engage in opposing behavior. Manfred Bleuler wants to explain all other difficulties in the schizophrenic life, including the thought process disorder, the affective problems, and the major accessory symptoms of hallucinations, delusions, and disorders of person, as secondary to the autism.

A hierarchy of signs and symptoms is necessarily based on

the clinician's theory that assumes that some symptoms are primary and some are secondary. Eugen Bleuler's classification is an excellent example of such a hierarchy (see Table 1).

Table 1. BLEULER'S CLASSIFICATION OF SYMPTOMS
OF SCHIZOPHRENIA

I. FUNDAMENTAL SYMPTOMS (present in every case):

    A. Disturbance of association.*
    B. Affective indifference and inappropriateness.
    C. Autism.
    D. Ambivalence.

II. ACCESSORY SYMPTOMS (may or may not be present at a given time in a given case):

    A. Hallucinations.
    B. Delusions.
    C. Disorders of person.
    D. Disorders of speech and writing.
    E. Somatic symptoms.*
    F. Catatonic symptoms.
    G. Acute symptoms consisting of:
        1. Melancholia, mania, catatonia, acute paranoia.
        2. Stunnedness (*Benommenheit*).*
        3. Confusion and incoherence.
        4. Twilight state.
        5. Stupor.
        6. Deliria.
        7. Fugue states.
        8. Fits of anger.
        9. Anniversary excitements.
       10. Dipsomania.

* Primary symptoms that are related to postulated diffusely organic process.

There are other descriptive systems used by clinicians whose classification of signs and symptoms is based on a statistical point of view. These clinicians make lists of those signs and symptoms that appear in all cases, in some cases, in 90 percent of cases, and so forth. They have the statistical bias that frequency of occurrence of a symptom is the preferred approach to defining a diagnostic category. This approach to diagnosis does not require speculation about etiology, nor does it create a hierarchy (other than a statistical hierarchy) in terms of importance of symptoms. An example of this approach is Kurt Schneider's classification of end-stage symptoms (see Table 2).

Table 2. SCHNEIDER'S CLASSIFICATION OF
END-STAGE SYMPTOMS OF SCHIZOPHRENIA*

I. FIRST-RANK SYMPTOMS:

    A. AUDIBLE THOUGHTS.
    The patient experiences auditory hallucinations with voices speaking his thoughts aloud. The voice and thought are seen as separate entities occurring within a few seconds of each other. They must be identical in content, although the sequence of their occurrence is immaterial.

    B. VOICES ARGUING.
    There are two or more hallucinatory voices in disagreement or in discussion. The subject is usually the patient, who is referred to in the third person.

    C. VOICES COMMENTING ON ONE'S ACTION.
    The content of the auditory hallucination is a description of the patient's activities as they occur.

    D. INFLUENCE PLAYING ON THE BODY, SOMATIC PASSIVITY.
    The patient is a passive and invariably a reluctant recipient of bodily sensations imposed on him by some external agency. Bodily change and external control must be present.

    E. THOUGHT WITHDRAWAL.
    The patient describes his thoughts being taken from his mind by some external force.

    F. THOUGHTS ASCRIBED TO OTHERS (thought insertion).
    The patient experiences thoughts that have the quality of not being his own and that are imposed on his passive mind by varied means.

    G. DIFFUSION OR BROADCASTING OF THOUGHTS.
    The patient has the experience that his thoughts are not confined within his own mind but escape to the external world where they may be experienced by all around.

    H. "MADE" IMPULSES.
    Impulses overcome the patient, and, while the impulse to carry out the act is not felt to be his own, the actual performance of the act is.

    I. "MADE" FEELINGS.
    The patient experiences feelings that do not seem to be his own but are imposed on him by some external source.

J. "Made" Volitional Acts.
   The patient feels his actions as being under the control of an external influence that initiates and directs his movements.

K. Delusional Perception.
   The delusion arises from a perception that is based on reality but to which the patient ascribes a private meaning. It is from this special meaning that the delusion is crystallized. The perception itself may be preceded by a delusional atmosphere.

II. SECOND-RANK SYMPTOMS:

A. Other forms of hallucinations.
B. Perplexity.
C. Depression.
D. Euphoric disorders of affect.
E. Emotional blunting.

ᵃ Abstracted from C. S. Mellor, *British Journal of Psychiatry*, 1970, *117*, 15–23.

There are other classifications. Parfitt (1956) lists signs and symptoms that he believes are present in all cases of schizophrenia (see Table 3).

Table 3. Parfitt's List of Signs and Symptoms
of Schizophrenia

1. Difficulty in thinking and expressing thoughts.
2. Reduction in ability to plan.
3. Difficulty in separating thoughts and events.
4. Failing ability to recognize absurdity.
5. Failing insight.
6. Reduced intelligence.
7. Reduced learning.

It becomes increasingly clear from these lists of descriptions that we are observing human beings who, by their illness and by the treatment imposed on them, are forced into certain life-styles that may account for some of their difficulties in living. The problems seen in chronic schizophrenic patients who have been hospitalized and isolated for a long period, problems formerly attributed to the result of chronic schizophrenia, turned out to be the result of chronic hospitalization and alienation from society. Many of the people who were observed to be extremely autistic, whose contact

with reality was severely impaired, and who engaged in idiosyncratic thinking and hebephrenic joking were simply responding to
having lived many years in the strange world of a mental hospital
back ward. Much of what was seen as deterioration or dementia
praecox turned out to be not the result of the illness but the result
of chronic treatment, chronic isolation, chronic alienation, and
chronically being in that peculiar sick role imposed by schizophrenia.

There is yet another group of psychiatrists (R. D. Laing and
others, 1965), who maintain that the manifestations of schizophrenia
are secondary to growth experience. In this growth experience, the
patient who is called *schizophrenic* is experimenting with various
approaches to the world around him. The schizophrenia is not an
illness but rather a manifestation of an awkward and disjointed
attempt at growth.

Existential psychiatrists are primarily concerned with how
each of us constructs his or her world in terms of the phenomenological categories. Schizophrenia is viewed by such psychiatrists as
secondary to alterations in time, space, and causality perception. The
individual creates the schizophrenic world in which he chooses to
live because of his perceptual and experiential disorder.

Our proposal for classifying the signs and symptoms of
schizophrenia begins with the understanding that a human being is
physically, psychologically, and socially a system within a system.
This system has a tendency to maintain balance and sameness
(homeostasis). This tendency to maintain sameness is particularly
true in regard to functions. As the individual develops dysfunctions,
he will tend to develop techniques and mechanisms to restitute for
these dysfunctions. He has the tendency to maximize his functions,
to restore his comfort, and to preserve his ability to live as economically as possible. It has long been understood that physical as
well as psychological signs and symptoms tend to be restitutive. The
body and the psyche respond to dysfunction by attempts at repair
and restoration. The pain, swelling, redness, and fever that are part
of physical disease are in fact defensive responses of tissue to inva-
sion by microorganisms. Similarly, the psychological defenses (adaptive capacities, coping mechanisms) are attempts at dealing with
anxiety and discomfort. These learned patterns are part of the
culture and part of the individual's psychological attempts at
restitution. When these restitutive attempts fail, when they become

excessive or uneconomical, then the coping mechanisms become signs and symptoms and are part of an illness. The resulting signs and symptoms are not random. They can be understood and they do make sense. The "choice" of symptoms is not conscious but is sensible. We can understand something about the problems for which restitution is attempted by looking at the symptom.

The psychiatric symptom of confabulation found in the brain-damaged individual can be viewed as an attempt to restitute for the discomfort of not being able to remember by "making up" facts to fill in. Delusions of grandeur, in which an individual ascribes great powers to himself, are attempts at restitution for feelings of severely impaired self-esteem. They repair the discomfort of being nobody and nothing. The delusion of being Jesus Christ or the Virgin Mary can be understood as a restitutive attempt at managing the discomfort of guilt. The auditory hallucination of hearing one's name called restitutes for no one knowing him, no one being interested in him, no one caring. Paranoid mechanisms restitute for feelings of insignificance. When one is paranoid, everyone looks at him, everyone is after him, everyone is concerned with him. This mechanism is the ultimate in restitutive megalomanic states.

Many signs and symptoms can be understood as restitutive for maintaining function and comfort and the continuity of life. Other signs and symptoms can be understood as physiological or psychological consequences of certain situations. For example, a chronic high level of anxiety has physiological sequelae that eventually will alter body chemistry in a measurable way. It is not that the altered body chemistry is part of the schizophrenia. Rather, it is part of the secondary consequence of a high level of unbound and unmanaged anxiety that one sees in the chronic schizophrenic person. These sequelae correspond to the malnutrition and poor physical hygiene seen in some schizophrenic persons who are not able to take care of themselves or who live in state hospital systems where the diet is inadequate and the public health conditions are atrocious. The old textbooks even stated that poor gum health and a high rate of tuberculosis were a part of schizophrenia.

Our view of schizophrenia is focused on a cluster of dysfunctions that seems to occur in all the patients included in this category of illness. Every patient who can be included in the category of schizophrenia, regardless of the subtype, shows three clusters of disabilities. These clusters are related to problems with *anxiety management, impairment of interpersonal relationship,* and the *failure of historicity.* All of the symptoms and signs that have been described by various clinicians seem to be comprehensible as secondary to these three disabilities. The symptoms of schizophrenia are either attempts at restitution or they are sequelae and consequences of these disabilities (see Table 4).

The high level of chronic anxiety caused by the impairment in anxiety management results in exhausting attempts at living. This enormous amount of free-floating anxiety secondarily causes the loose associations found in many schizophrenic patients. Even in a nonschizophrenic individual a high level of anxiety seems to bring about an impairment of thought processes indistinguishable from loose associations. The difference between the normal and the schizophrenic individual in respect to thought process is that the schizophrenic individual has loose associations in situations that ordinarily do not carry with them a high degree of anxiety: for example, the ordinary functions of everyday life. The loose associations of the schizophrenic person are not distinguishable from the loose associations of the normal person occurring during severe anxiety states.

Let us look at these three disabilities to begin to form a complete picture of the schizophrenic patient and his life. All of the signs and symptoms that we see in schizophrenic human beings, all of the difficulties they experience in the process of living, all of the peculiarities of life-style can be understood as the natural outcome of these three nuclear clusters. The failure of interpersonal relationship, the failure of anxiety management, and the failure of historicity have recognizable consequences. The consequences, as well as the disabilities, result in attempts at restitution both for function and for comfort. These attempts are usually partially or totally unsuccessful and lead to further symptoms.

Consequential Signs and Symptoms

The failure and expense of anxiety management typically seen in the schizophrenic person results in a high degree of free-floating anxiety that is seen in all such patients and observed as part

Table 4. CLASSIFICATION OF SIGNS AND SYMPTOMS

Nuclear Disabilities	Consequential Symptoms	Restitutive Symptoms
Failure of anxiety management	1. Tiredness and exhaustion 2. Loose associations 3. Communication difficulty caused by lack of discernible logic 4. Fragile adjustment 5. Affective lability 6. Failure to learn from experience 7. Confusion 8. Disorganized behavior 9. Amotivationality—ambivalence—ambitendency 10. Impaired reality contact	1. Panneurosis 2. Ritualistic behavior 3. Idiosyncratic thought processes 4. Suicide 5. Delusions 6. Hallucinations 7. Affective indifference and inappropriateness 8. Reduced functional intelligence 9. Reduced functional learning 10. Involvement with drugs and alcoholism 11. Feelings of being out of control or in control of someone else
Failure of interpersonal transactions	1. Impaired self-boundaries 2. Feelings of emptiness and nothingness 3. Impaired flow of time 4. Impairment of reality contact 5. Low self-esteem	1. Withdrawal 2. Autism—impaired reality contact 3. Megalomania 4. Delusions of grandeur 5. Paranoid symptoms 6. Hypochondriasis 7. Bizarre behavior 8. Hopelessness 9. Polymorphous sexual perversion 10. Difficulty in separating thoughts and events
Failure of historicity	1. Feelings of emptiness and nothingness 2. Impaired self-esteem 3. No past, no future 4. No flow of time 5. No sense of person 6. No continuity of person 7. Ambivalence and ambitendency 8. Failure to have "learned" from experience 9. Fragility of therapeutic relationship, which needs constant nourishment	1. Filling life with nongoal-oriented activity 2. Enslavement in the present moment of action 3. Unwillingness to plan or commit to action 4. Living at the periphery of life 5. Disconnection of the personal world from the surrounding world

of their life-style (see Table 4). The consequences of always being anxious in even the most ordinary circumstances of everyday existence are clearly visible. Such patients show a tiredness and exhaustion that cannot be explained in terms of their physical state or the tasks in which they have engaged. Just getting through the day is exhausting. Anyone who has had some anxious days can empathize with this difficulty. Going through the day with a high level of anxiety is like walking down the street with a 200-pound suitcase in each hand. An ordinary walk becomes a drudgery, each step is a terrible ordeal. One finishes the day in paralyzing tiredness, seeking sleep and rest like a drug addict seeking his next fix. And then, unfortunately, the sleep is not restful because even there a massive amount of unhandled anxiety disturbs the physiological and psychological restitution. Such failure of anxiety management leads to clearly visible symptoms in the life of the person who has schizophrenia. His fragile adjustment, where minor events become major crises, is an example of his resourcelessness. This fragility causes the affective lability shown by so many of these patients.

Other difficulties that are a consequence of the failure of anxiety management include the patient's inability to attend to present reality and therefore the failure to learn from experience. This failure results in confusion, disorganized behavior, and impaired reality contact. The failure of anxiety management has as a consequence two of Eugen Bleuler's fundamental symptoms of schizophrenia. The loose associations (a thought process disorder) are found consistently in schizophrenic persons who are always carrying a great deal of anxiety even when there seems to be no external cause for such anxiety. These loose associations result in the communication difficulty that Feighner (1972) has described as basic to schizophrenia. The lack of clearly definable logic is caused by the idiosyncratic thought processes.

The second fundamental symptom that can be understood as consequential to the failure of anxiety management is ambivalence demonstrated as an immobilizing amotivationality. Ambivalence is part of being human, but to be immobilized by the ambivalence, to be caught up in the ambitendency of two opposing pressures for action, to be, like the Cartesian donkey, stuck between two haystacks while starving to death, is truly schizophrenic. The confusion, the disorganized behavior, and the impaired reality contact are also in part consequences of the failure of anxiety management.

Restitutional Signs and Symptoms

The normal mechanism of living organisms is restitution for disturbances, discomfort, and failure of function. In an attempt to restitute for the painful dysfunctional state of failure of anxiety management and its consequences, the individual develops other symptoms (see Table 4).

The panneurosis seen in the schizophrenic human being is typical and represents the multiple and unsuccessful attempts at managing the anxiety. In this attempt, the individual develops a multitude of "neurotic" symptoms without ever successfully managing the anxiety. He may be obsessive, compulsive, amnesic, depressed, and hysterical all at the same time. He uses all of the mechanisms of managing anxiety, yet none of them works and all of them result in symptoms. The content of delusions and hallucinations is an attempt to restitute for the discomfort of the anxiety. The individual projects his own feelings onto others in an attempt to make himself more comfortable. He "manages" his loneliness and isolation by hearing voices; he handles his feelings of inadequacy and hopelessness by developing ideas of grandiosity. We can see that symptoms including delusions and hallucinations, ritualistic behavior, involvement with drugs and alcoholism, idiosyncratic thought processes, suicidal rumination and behavior, the feeling of helplessness and being out of control or in the control of someone else are all attempts at restitution. The mechanism of symptom formation is frequently the consequence of the failing anxiety management, but the content of the symptom is related to an attempt at restitution. The failure to manage anxiety, for example, has the consequence of a high level of anxiety leading to loose associations. The loose associations lead to difficulty in communication with others caused by lack of logical or understandable organization in the communication. This failure in communication leads to an attempt at restitution seen in the development of very personal thought processes that become the foundation of the individual's craziness.

A similar sequence of disability, consequential symptoms, and restitution is seen in the development of the flat affect. The failing anxiety management results in the affective lability that is so painful for the schizophrenic person and his environment. This discomfort is dealt with by behavior characterized by the affective indifference and inappropriateness thought by Eugen Bleuler to be one of the fundamental symptoms of schizophrenia.

The second disability, the failure of interpersonal relationships characterized by clumsiness and inability to conduct the interpersonal transaction for the desired outcome, also has serious consequences. We observe these consequences in the clinical picture of the schizophrenic individual, in the impaired borders of self, feelings of emptiness and nothingness, and feelings of low self-esteem. The tremendously impaired self-boundaries lead to further symptoms, so that the patient really does not know what is inside and what is outside, what his thoughts are, or what the thoughts and words of others might be. From each interpersonal transaction the patient comes away feeling worse about himself, worse about the world. Each time he has less faith in his fellow man, less faith in the world in which he lives, and no faith in the earth on which he stands. This condition further increases anxiety and adds to the problems previously discussed in relation to that cluster of disabilities. Most nonschizophrenic persons have available the use of interpersonal transactions as a technique of managing anxiety. The schizophrenic individual does not. It is in this way that disability in interpersonal transactions leads to increased difficulty in the other two disabilities, anxiety management and failing historicity.

The consequences of the failing interpersonal relationships seen in the impairment of self-boundaries and self-esteem are terribly painful. Recent research with sensory deprivation shows that each of us maintains much of his self-boundary by bouncing signals off the world around us and by defining ourselves in relationship to others. The maintenance of the self is possible only in relationship to others. A consequence of the impairment of self-boundaries when interpersonal relationships are severely damaged, painful, unsuccessful, and withdrawn from includes the terminal eleven first-rank symptoms of schizophrenia described by Kurt Schneider. When the patient can no longer differentiate between his own and others' thoughts, fantasies, wishes, and dreams, when he can no longer differentiate between what he has done and what he has only thought or wished or fantasized, then we see the end state of the schizophrenic condition characterized by Schneider's first-rank symptoms.

To deal with all of these consequences of the failing interpersonal relationship, human beings make restitutive attempts to reduce the pain and awareness, and to explain the dysfunction. They attempt to create meaning out of situations in which there seems to be no meaning. These restitutive attempts then become symptoms, including withdrawal and autism. Autism seems to us to be a restitutive attempt to deal with the pain and agony of such failing adventures in interpersonal relationships. Some other of the major psychotic symptoms can also be understood as attempts at restitution. These symptoms include the megalomania and delusions of grandeur that are restitutive attempts at dealing with severely impaired self-esteem. Bizarre behavior frequently is used as an explanation for impaired interpersonal relationship, thus making meaning out of nonmeaning. Polymorphous sexual perversion represents a clumsy restitutional attempt, and hopelessness and catatonia become a final and bizarre way in which the individual removes himself from the arena of interpersonal transactions in which he suffers so much pain and failure.

The third disability cluster, failing historicity, further aggravates the other two disabilities. Because the individual who lives with schizophrenia cannot draw on his own personal lived history as a source of experience for making judgments, having faith in the future, or experiencing the continuity of life, his difficulties in managing anxiety and in interpersonal transactions are even more aggravated. Because each day the patient must get up to face the world as though it were the first day of his life, each interpersonal transaction is fraught with even more difficulty than it would be if he could recall prior similar or different transactions. Because he must meet each minor challenge of the day, each pebble in the path of his life, without being able to draw on prior experience to make decisions or to move into action, his anxiety level is heightened and his ability to use anxiety management techniques is diminished.

This failure of historicity has the consequence that the patient feels empty, feels nothing. This feeling further impairs his self-esteem, further disconnects him from his past, and makes it more difficult for him to conceptualize the future. He has no experience of the flow of time. He has no personal self that has continuity and with which he can meet the day. Without being able to fall back on personal experience from which to make decisions, he is immobilized in ambivalence and ambitendency. It seems as though he cannot learn from experience, even though he has no learning difficulty. Further consequences include the difficulty in planning and commitment to a course of action described by Parfitt as always present in schizophrenic life. The disconnection with the past and the future, the failing experience of the flow of time, enslaves the person in the present moment of action. He therefore engages in behavior that appears not oriented toward a goal and not related to his own needs or wishes. Restitutive attempts are made by the patient to deal with this failing. He fills his life with activity. He produces delusions and hallucinations to connect him in the present moment with a past and a future that does not exist. He invents grand schemes of either benevolent or malevolent intent as his paranoia becomes an attempt at restituting for the unbearable agony of having no past and no future and of being a prisoner of the moment.

Chapter 3

⧁⧁⧁⧁⧁⧁⧁⧁

The Problem of Anxiety

A nxiety, the psychological equivalent of pain, is characterized by a feeling of dread. It is a vague fear that is not related to specific situations or objects. Anxiety is part of the human condition. It is part of the experience of every human being. However, for the person who suffers from schizophrenia, the problem of anxiety is an entirely different matter.

Nonschizophrenic human beings learn to handle their anxiety in a variety of ways. How each of us handles his anxiety is characteristic of him and becomes his personality. The ways in which we manage our anxiety is something we learn in childhood. The patterns of anxiety management for each of us tend to remain fairly constant throughout adulthood. For example, one individual may handle his anxiety in sequence first by repression, then by sublimation and obsession, and finally by projection. Another individual may use the same mechanisms of managing anxiety but in a very different sequence. The sequence of anxiety-managing techniques used by the individual is one way of describing personality. No matter how each of us manages anxiety, we attempt to do so without using all of our available life energy. Our goal is to bind the anxiety in such a way that we can get on with the process of living in comfort and with some degree of freedom. The more integrated one is as a person, the more he can tolerate anxiety; some persons even have a zest for anxiety.

When anxiety becomes excessive and overwhelming, the ways of managing anxiety may become symptoms. Normal techniques of managing anxiety become the symptoms of neurosis.

The ordinary techniques of binding and managing anxiety do not work for the person with schizophrenia. His attempts at anxiety binding are tremendously expensive; little energy is left over for living life. Those individuals who have the schizophrenic cluster of disabilities show a failure of anxiety management and demonstrate an uneconomical, disastrously expensive attempt at managing anxiety. The failure of anxiety management is directly responsible for a number of the signs and symptoms thought to be characteristic of schizophrenia. With a high level of free-floating anxiety, even nonschizophrenic individuals develop some difficulties in thinking, such as loose association. (Loose associations abound in examination papers by undergraduate students who are anxious about their exams.) The schizophrenic patient has loose associations most of the time. Since he must live with intolerably high levels of anxiety because of his failing and expensive anxiety management techniques, his loose associations (thought by Bleuler to be pathognomonic of schizophrenia) are simply the result of chronic high levels of free-floating anxiety. The thought process disorder is a manifestation of the problems of anxiety in schizophrenic patients.

Another aspect of symptoms resulting from the problems of anxiety management is the exhaustion seen in many schizophrenic patients. One can follow a patient through his usual day to recognize that simply living (sleeping, getting up, eating, getting dressed, getting out, getting back in, getting undressed, and going to sleep) involves so much anxiety that human beings with schizophrenia are exhausted just "getting through." To watch a schizophrenic person live his life is exhausting even for the observer.

There has been considerable discussion about the nature of anxiety in schizophrenic patients. Clinicians have debated whether schizophrenic anxiety is different from normal anxiety. No one has been able to demonstrate any difference in the nature of the anxiety of individuals who have schizophrenia from the anxiety of those who have other types of difficulties in living. Anxiety in schizophrenic patients has the same painful discomfort it has in others. It is the same feeling of dread, the same pervasive psychological pain, the same vague, unattached discomfort. It seems to result in the same physiological concomitants that can be objectively measured and subjectively experienced and self-reported. Anxiety in the lives of schizophrenic people has the same quality of signaling conflict and apprehension as it does in others. What is different in the lives of schizophrenic people is how the anxiety is handled, how effectively it is managed, how much of it remains free-floating, how readily it is aroused, and how much energy it takes to bind it. We can also see the difference by the level of exhaustion that dealing with constant anxiety brings with inadequate tools and inadequate systems. The fire that is fought with a strong, large hose connected to a fire hydrant is no different from the fire fought by spitting on it. The fires are exactly the same, but the consequences are markedly different. The anxiety is the same; it is how it is handled in schizophrenic lives that is different.

What causes the difficulty in managing anxiety in human existences plagued by schizophrenia? There is a great deal of debate about this question, though nothing is known about it. We will present some of these speculations in Part II when we summarize theories of etiology. These failures in techniques of managing anxiety must be attributable to failure in learning techniques, to inborn defects that cannot be repaired, or to faulty techniques that have been caused by problems in living. There is considerable evidence that newborn infants vary a great deal from each other in their ability to experience, tolerate, and manage stress. Observations in a nursery for newborns shows that the infant at the time of birth already has a "personality" in terms of his excitability, irritability, physiological response mechanisms, arousal states, and so on. Whether these differences in the newborn are inherited differences in the nervous system or other tissue systems or whether they are at birth already the result of the experiences the infant had in the intrauterine environment is still in question. We know that the intrauterine environment influences the behavior of the fetus and that some learning does go on there. But members of families tend to inherit arousal patterns, energy patterns, and simple behavior response patterns.

The study of newborn infants, as well as of growth and development during the first few years of life, demonstrates that techniques of managing anxiety are taught in the family during the earliest days of extrauterine life. During child rearing, by behavior modification and identification, the young child learns how to deal with his feelings and how to cope with the discomfort of anxiety. If the modeling behavior of the adults is consistent with the techniques of managing anxiety that are reinforced through reward and punishment, the child develops a very consistent pattern of anxiety management early in his life. If these influences are confused, contradictory, or inconsistent, the techniques of managing anxiety in the child become ineffective and chaotic. It also seems that anxiety is more easily aroused in children who later develop schizophrenic difficulties in living. This ease of arousal may be part of the other two primary disabilities that a schizophrenic person experiences in his life, namely the difficulty with historicity and the difficulty with his interpersonal relationships. Each of us has difficulty in living. Difficulties in living are associated with heightened levels of anxiety. Even in normal lives these heightened levels of anxiety may lead to temporary malfunction and symptom formation. In schizophrenic existences, the arousal of anxiety is mercurial and excessive, while at the same time the means to manage the anxiety are inadequate and exhausting. In the normal course of human existence, difficulties in living seem to cluster at specific problem periods. These periods include the time of adolescence or middle age, menopause, or retirement, when we come to grips with our own frailty and mortality. Problem periods also include the time of major commitments such as graduation, marriage, parenthood, or divorce. A schizophrenic has to face these same difficulties. It is at such times that acute exacerbations of the clinical condition occur. This tendency often leads to incorrect diagnoses. Many women who are diagnosed as suffering from postpartum depression are in fact suffering from acute exacerbation of a chronic schizophrenic process that has been precipitated by the stress of facing parenthood, by the physiological changes after childbirth, and by the frightening feelings of inadequacy to the tasks of parenthood.

A schizophrenic human being has much unbound anxiety. He also has a lifelong pattern of clumsy interpersonal relationships that usually end in disaster. When he enters into new relationships, his interpersonal ability is decreased even further by a high level of anxiety, which in turn is increased by his long series of interpersonal failures. This state leads to further failure, more anxiety, more disorganization, and more symptom formation. Since anxiety management techniques are learned, and since anxiety management is facilitated by having available the history of personally lived experiences of having managed anxiety or not managed anxiety, the failure of historicity adds further to the difficulty in anxiety management (see Chapter 5). The patient "has no experience" to draw on and comes anew to each new life situation. Each time the schizophrenic person has to do all of the "work." The problem becomes circular because the increased level of anxiety interferes with the development of historicity. When the individual is so anxious that he is not open to experience, and is withdrawn from reality contact, then the events in his life have even less chance of sticking to his ribs and becoming part of his life history.

The failure of anxiety management thus results in the signs and symptoms that are usually associated with making the diagnosis of schizophrenia.

Ambivalence is part of the human condition. But resolving ambivalence is something that is much more difficult for the schizophrenic human than for the nonschizophrenic person. You and I can resolve our ambivalence in some way and make a commitment to choices. The schizophrenic patient is immobilized. This immobilization is related to the high levels of anxiety that overcharge any commitment to choice. The autism that both Eugen and Manfred

Bleuler describe as a fundamental symptom of schizophrenia may also be the result of the high levels of anxiety. When a human being is constantly anxious, when he is exhausted by experiencing these constant high levels of anxiety and by his attempts at managing them, he has less energy left over for contact with reality. He withdraws from reality, he withdraws into himself, and he becomes autistic. The affective flattening often described by observers of schizophrenic patients can be understood as the withdrawal of psychological and life energy from the interpersonal situation. The patient has nothing left over after the faulty and expensive attempt at managing anxiety.

The symptom described as *panneurosis,* the condition in which many normal techniques of managing anxiety are used at the same time, is a clinical condition characteristic of certain stages of schizophrenia. In this condition the human being is depressed, withdrawn, obsessive, compulsive, paranoid (projecting), and somatizing; he has hysterical symptoms and none of them works. In the area of sexuality, we see the picture of polymorphous sexual perversion. The patient, frequently in a short span of time, enters into heterosexual, homosexual, exhibitionistic, voyeuristic, sadistic, and masochistic relationships. All of them are inadequate. None leads to sexual satisfaction. All of them culminate in interpersonal disasters.

The failure of anxiety management also results in impaired self-esteem. The human being who is always anxious, who never feels effective and successful, who enters into each situation knowing that he is going to lose, obviously cannot develop a self-concept from which he can draw solace and comfort. It was on this symptom, the impaired self-esteem, that Harry Stack Sullivan focused his interest. He saw this problem as the major issue of the schizophrenic life.

Other signs and symptoms resulting from the failure of anxiety management include the experience of dread and fear, the fragility of adjustment, and the brittle integrity of personality. Minor crises precipitate major dysfunction. A broken shoelace may precipitate a major disorganization and crisis. Such fragility is part of the schizophrenic human being's personality even when the overt major clinical symptoms seem in good remission.

The failure to learn from experience is in part the result of the high level of anxiety with which the individual lives at all times. The confusion of the acute schizophrenic state seems to be a direct result of the disorganization of consciousness occurring under the weight of excessive free-floating anxiety. The acutely schizophrenic patient can appear so confused that on occasion he may resemble the patient with an acute organic condition. Similarly, the chronic patient, particularly one who has experienced many years of chronic hospitalization, may be confused to the extent of seeming organically injured. In the old days, when it was common practice to hospitalize chronic schizophrenic patients for thirty, forty, or fifty years, one could go on the back ward of any state hospital and see patients who appeared organic. Their confusion was caused by years of social isolation, but some of the confusion of the acutely schizophrenic patient may be caused by the disorganizing effect of a chronic high level of anxiety.

Constantly living with high levels of anxiety also has physiological consequences. We know that the physiological concomitants of anxiety vary from person to person, but generally these concomitants include tension. Such chronic tension results in a wide variety of somatic symptoms. These symptoms may then reinforce the generalized hypochondriases seen in schizophrenia. The outcome may eventually be the somatic delusions seen in some schizophrenic lives. Often the somatic delusion begins with the minor and normal physiological concomitants of anxiety. The hypochondriases seen in some schizophrenic patients may be pervasive and so misleading that some patients who suffer primarily from chronic schizophrenia end up as polysurgical addicts. They have a whole series of vague physical complaints that lead to surgical interventions such as laparotomies and removal of the gall bladder, teeth, appendix, and female organs. They go from doctor to doctor without responding to medical or surgical intervention.

The constant high level of anxiety with its associated skeletal muscle tension further aggravates the psychologically based physical clumsiness and ritualistic movements occasionally seen in patients who live schizophrenic lives. This clumsiness is not the same as the phenothiazine-induced extrapyramidal effects. One sees the stiffness and ritualistic movement and clumsiness even in patients who do not take phenothiazine. Such patients look like wooden human beings, their extremities moving as though on a string, bending jerkily at the joints.

The high level of unmanaged and unbound anxiety often leads to disorganization of perceptual processes '(hallucinations), to misinterpretations of reality '(paranoia)', to thought mechanism disorders (delusions), and to behavioral disorganization (crazy behavior).

So pervasive is the disorganization caused by the high level of unmanaged anxiety that most of Schneider's first-rank symptoms of schizophrenia can be understood as consequences of the basic failure of anxiety management.

The exhaustion of the person has clinical consequences in tiredness and lethargy, lack of zest for life, and amotivationality. One of the most difficult and frustrating aspects of treating a schizophrenic patient is his amotivational state. The pain and agony of the dreaded emptiness of schizophrenic existence would convince anyone that there must be motivation to change to a state of more comfort as long as the person is alive. However, because not much energy is left over to engage in therapy and rehabilitation activities, the patient often appears amotivational.

The exhaustion from carrying a high level of anxiety is an experience that most human beings have had at some time in their lives. The exhaustion can be greater than the exhaustion from physical activity. Many patients seek medical attention for that exhaustion and resort to vitamins, stimulants, diets, sleep cures, and so forth to manage the uncomfortable tiredness. On occasion, the exhaustion can be so paralyzing and so great that the patient may want to escape from both the unbearable high level of anxiety and the unbearable tiredness by suicide. Suicide is a serious risk in schizophrenic lives.

Once the clinician understands the problem of anxiety in the schizophrenic existence, a rational · approach to treatment emerges. There are three approaches involved in helping the individual to manage his problem with anxiety. First, we help him to organize his life situation by identifying the pebbles in life's path over which he stumbles. We help him to avoid as much conflict and stress as possible to avoid triggering increased anxiety. Second, we train and teach him techniques of managing anxiety that suit him, that are available to him, and that are tolerated by society. Third, we offer him medication to help him to manage anxiety. There are specific techniques for each of these treatment approaches. With proper treatment, the patient can manage his anxiety effectively enough to have the opportunity to function and to get enjoyment out of living life.

Chapter 4

✄✄✄✄✄✄✄✄

Failure of Interpersonal Relationships

The arena of interpersonal transactions and relationships is the most sensitive of all to psychological and behavioral disturbances. Before a major difficulty in thinking, a gross behavioral abnormality or major affective disorganization is apparent, interpersonal relationships show the effect of psychological disturbances and disorganization. Even in healthy and neurotic persons, the interpersonal arena is most taxing and therefore shows the most effect of temporary life stress. The interpersonal difficulties seen in the patient with schizophrenia are qualitatively and quantitatively quite different from those found in other persons. The cluster of interpersonal disabilities is characterized by the clumsiness that uniformly leads to a disastrous outcome of the transaction. This disastrous interpersonal outcome is repeated over and over in the life of a schizophrenic person until finally he gives up and no longer attempts to relate interpersonally. From each transaction he comes away feeling worthless and hopeless about the possibility of a satisfying human relationship. From each transaction comes a further rupture of basic faith in his fellow man.

A somewhat similar interpersonal situation, one that helps us to understand the schizophrenic world, has been described and observed in individuals who have survived concentration camps. The condition of postconcentration-camp personality defect has been observed as a basic inability to ever again develop a trusting relationship with fellow human beings. This basic rupture of faith results from being exposed to members of the human race who do not share any of the assumptions that human beings make about other human beings. The schizophrenic individual is very much in the same kind of situation. He is unable to develop trust and faith enough to relate openly or to take the risk of the interpersonal transaction that is always necessary in a relationship. As each new interpersonal transaction fails for the patient, his lack of trust and of faith, the knowledge of certain interpersonal failure, and the disastrous outcome are reinforced into his motivational system.

Much has been said about this basic failure in the lives of schizophrenic individuals. Symptoms such as withdrawal and the amotivational state are secondary consequences of this disability. Since all treatment occurs in the matrix of the interpersonal relationship, regardless of whether it consists of persuading the patient to take his medication, of psychotherapy, milieu manipulation or hospitalization, this failure of faith presents a major difficulty in treating schizophrenia. The helpful management of the patient depends on the doctor-patient relationship. The difficulties the therapist experiences in treating the schizophrenic person occur because the means by which he administers treatment is impaired by the disability of the patient. This situation is like having to administer intravenous medication to someone who has sclerosed veins. The patient needs what the therapist has to give, and wants what he has to offer, but the therapist cannot get it to the patient. In the treatment of physical disease we resort to heroic measures to get the proper treatment to patients and we have to do the same in dealing with schizophrenic patients. The usual interpersonal transactions do not seem to work. We must resort to heroic measures to form and maintain a relationship in order to administer treatment.

The cluster of difficulties caused by the disabilities in the interpersonal relationships is characterized by two aspects. The first of these is that the relationships are clumsily handled. The second is that the outcome is never what is intended, and is always disastrous for the patient.

It is important that we understand these clusters of disabilities in more detail. Clumsiness leads to much of the difficulty that the schizophrenic individual experiences in his life. His intent is constantly misinterpreted by others. A frightened, disorganized human being, who is in panic and who reaches out for help in a clumsy way, is often seen as hostile and aggressive. Because of the misunderstood reaching out, the patient does not get his rescue but is treated as though he were antagonistic. His situation is much like that of the drowning person who chokes the lifeguard. A disorganized, frightened, schizophrenic patient walks down the hall and tries to reach out to a representative of the helping situation such as a nurse, a social worker, a doctor, or any other fellow human being. He clumsily brushes against the person and perhaps grasps him. The other person thinks the patient is attacking him and responds by yelling for help, increasing medication, putting the patient in restraints, making a note on the chart saying the patient is hostile and aggressive, secluding the patient, or running away. All of these responses are a disastrous outcome of the interpersonal transaction in which the patient has reached out for help and found himself responded to as though he were aggressive. In fact, he manages to get himself rejected. The patient's clumsiness has resulted in a disaster for himself. There are numerous examples of the many interpersonal misadventures seen in the lives of schizophrenic persons. A patient might be aware of feeling warm, loving emotions toward another human being; he approaches and wants to express these, but in his clumsiness he makes a sarcastic remark. The other person responds to this overture by also being sarcastic and rejecting the patient. One can see that the clumsy attempts at relationships by schizophrenic persons make them come away from each interpersonal transaction feeling worse about themselves and worse about the possibility of attempting another such adventure. Their self-esteem is further impaired and their ability to engage in future interpersonal relationships is decreased. The amotivational condition observed in schizophrenic human beings, their inability to get themselves going, to enter into things, and to be part of the social space, is the result of the hopelessness about the possible success of their clumsy interpersonal transactions. As each interpersonal venture fails, the patient's anxiety level is increased, and thus his ability to respond appropriately in the next interpersonal transaction is even further impaired.

The interpersonal misadventures and clumsy transactions become reciprocal causes in a downward spiral of function accompanied by increasing anxiety. When the schizophrenic person wants to express love, he cannot get the point across; when he wants to express anger, he is not taken seriously; when he tries to display his agony and despair, others do not understand or laugh at him; when he attempts intimacy, he is injured; when he wants nurture, he is rebuffed; when he wants acceptance, he is rejected. Finally, the spiral of misadventure, bad outcome, failure, rejections, and further impairment of self-esteem leads to total withdrawal and unwillingness to relate to anyone. This condition is made even more difficult by the failure of historicity (see Chapter 5). Since each interpersonal transaction begins anew and since to some extent the patient cannot draw on his prior history, each such transaction is entered into anew with a vague feeling of prior failure but with no learned experience on which to base an interpersonal attempt. Whatever successful interpersonal relationships have been experienced are not available as living history offering a basis for functioning.

To provide rehabilitation, retraining, and remotivation in the interpersonal sphere is one of the most difficult tasks facing the therapist in the treatment of the schizophrenic patient. As the treatment is based on a therapeutic relationship, it is a task that must be accomplished. Special techniques, which we discuss in further detail in the section on treatment interventions, do allow the formation of a relationship. This relationship, like a controlled laboratory situation, can be used to teach the patient how to relate with some success to avoid interpersonal failure. The therapeutic relationship must then be used to help the patient generalize to his life outside of the treatment situation. The patient learns to go through the motions of a relationship. Later he can commit himself enough to try again and to risk some feelings.

A schizophrenic person whose interpersonal clumsiness and misadventures make him difficult for others is even more difficult for himself. He has a tendency to retreat to an empty world populated by his fantasies and unrelated to real people. A patient told me that to him the world is peopled as to others the house is furnished. He has to learn how to use them and be comfortable with them but he cannot relate in any way other than he does to furniture.

There is much speculation on what causes this cluster of disabilities in interpersonal transactions in schizophrenic patients. A number of theories are discussed in the section on etiology. Whether it is a failure of learning, a traumatic or unsatisfying relationship in the earliest months of life, a genetic defect or a failure of maturation of the nervous system in the early years, or biochemical or anatomical is unknown at this time. But all schizophrenic patients have this difficulty, and this cluster of disabilities is closely related to the disabilities of anxiety management and to the failure of historicity.

These disabilities in the interpersonal sphere lead to significant problems in the life of the schizophrenic person. He is misinterpreted, misunderstood, and rejected; in turn, he misunderstands and misinterprets the response of others. The pain and agony of such interpersonal misadventures are the basis of some of the major symptoms that have been associated with schizophrenia. Autism, restitutive hallucinations and delusions, and fuzziness of self-boundaries in which the patient confuses inside and outside are all part of the response to interpersonal pain and misadventure.

Although interpersonal difficulties are always a concomitant of emotional problems, the interpersonal disasters in schizophrenia are qualitatively and quantitatively distinct. Its ultimate expression is the catatonic stupor, the waxy flexibility, and the chronic hebephrenic patient who relates to nothing except his own world populated by fantasy figures over which he has mastery.

Chapter 5

※※※※※※※※

Failure of Historicity

Historicity is that quality in human existence that makes our lived personal history available to us to draw on for the conduct of our lives. In nonschizophrenic human beings, this lived, available history makes it possible for each of us to risk new situations, new relationships, and new experiences. We enter into situations with certain assumptions about others in the transaction; these assumptions give us some confidence and self-esteem.

In the schizophrenic existence, this lived history seems not to be available. This lack is by no means caused by a memory deficit, since the schizophrenic person does not have impaired memory. It is not that the facts are unavailable to the schizophrenic or that they cannot be recalled; it is rather that personal lived history is not available to draw on as a source of experience. It is as though prior relationships and experiences have gone right through the person. They have not stuck to his ribs. Each new relationship has to be entered into anew. Each new activity is taking place for the first time. Thus the day becomes long and strenuous. The schizophrenic human being enters into situations and relationships like a new-born infant, having no experience, no way of predicting, no way of using shared assumptions with others in the transaction.

There are other types of patients who, like the schizophrenic person, do not seem to "learn from experience." In the neurotic patient, for example, there is a repetition compulsion by which the patient repeats a pathological pattern of behavior as a way of dealing with unconscious conflict. But he has his lived history available to him. In fact, the predominance of much earlier his-torical events causes the repetitive behavior unrelated to present reality. The schizophrenic patient does not have repetition com-pulsions but, rather, more random behavior related to the present and totally cut off from his own history.

Such a failure of historicity poses a serious problem for therapy. Since within the matrix of the treatment transaction there must be the available history of prior appointments and the anticipa-tion of the future, the schizophrenic existence and the therapist at-tempting to intervene in that existence present major difficulties. Because there seems to be no remaining lived history at any one moment, when the experience stops it is as though none of it stayed with the schizophrenic person. This pattern is clearly seen in the problems of treatment. Even if the therapist has developed a good relationship with a schizophrenic patient by meticulous attention to the details of therapy, including keeping appointments, being on time, returning phone calls, even over a period of ten years, when something goes awry, such as an appointment being missed, it is as though the previous ten years never existed. The patient responds to having been let down and disappointed by the therapist as though there were no "long-term," reliable, prior relationship. He responds by "knowing" again that he can trust no one and that once again he has been rejected by his fellow man. The fact that for ten years the therapist has been reliable and consistent and available seems to have little bearing on the response. It is such failure of historicity that is so discouraging for many beginning therapists who first treat schizophrenic persons.

When a reality situation makes it necessary to transfer a schizophrenic patient to another therapist, it is usually much harder on the former therapist than on his patient. The schizophrenic patient can transfer over easily to a new therapist, while the therapist he has left may mourn the loss of his patient. Such observations led the early psychoanalyst to say that schizophrenic people do not form a transference. This judgment is not true at all. They form an intense and often a very dependent relationship with the therapist that is mercurial in its swings from positive to negative feelings.

The failure of historicity also has an effect on the other two nuclear clusters of disabilities, the failure of anxiety management and the difficulty in interpersonal relationships. In anxiety management, much of what most of us do is based on prior experience. Because of the failure of historicity the schizophrenic human being must begin each anxiety management anew. He cannot draw on yesterday's or last week's technique of handling his anxious moments. He cannot use the pattern of defenses in the same order in which he has used them before. Rather, he must experiment anew each time. The person cannot develop confidence, because he approaches each situation from the beginning. He does not remember that a year ago he handled his anxiety successfully, because he has no available history. His self-esteem is impaired as he enters into each transaction essentially without tried defenses.

In relation to the schizophrenic individual's problem with interpersonal relationships, the failure of historicity makes each new relationship the first and only one. He is unable to draw on his prior relationships and he has no faith in himself or in the world around him. The complexities of the interpersonal transaction each time must be handled for the first time. Nothing can be taken on faith. Each human interaction is a chance meeting with a totally unpredictable outcome involving new techniques of anxiety management.

The failure of historicity in the schizophrenic condition results in certain signs and symptoms. These include the feelings of emptiness and nothingness, the impaired self-esteem, the lack of flow of time with no past and no future, the enslavement in the present moment, the failure to learn from experience, the difficulty with ego boundaries and body image, and the difficulty in using the helping relationship. If I had to choose a difficulty as being primary in schizophrenia, I would propose that the failure of historicity is the most basic defect, though in fact it is only one of the three nuclear clusters of disabilities.

The failure of historicity results in an important problem for the schizophrenic person. Because his flow of time is altered and on occasion totally interrupted, his past is not available to him nor is his future open. When a person does not experience the flow of time, he is literally imprisoned in the present moment. He is a victim of whatever occurs. He has no past to buffer the interpretation and understanding of the experience. He has no future to serve as an anticipatory affect propelling him through the present. He is stuck in the present, in the moment of action.

Lived time is experienced as flowing. The flow of time is altered by states of pathology. For example, in severe depression the past overwhelms the future. In the manic patient, with his flight of ideas, the future totally overwhelms both the present and the past. But in the schizophrenic human being, the flow has stopped. He cannot experience anticipation, waiting, hoping, or expecting. All of these anticipatory affects that ordinarily influence the present moment are not available to modify the situation.

One of the important and difficult tasks of treatment becomes the reestablishment of the flow of time. A number of techniques have been developed that will be discussed in more detail. Essentially, these techniques consist of arranging concrete experiences with the patient in the therapeutic transaction that allow him to establish the flow of time from past through present to future. The simple device of giving an appointment slip for the next appointment is a concrete example of bringing the future to bear on the present. The patient may not have faith that the future will ever come, but he does have an appointment slip that shows him that the therapist has faith and plans his life accordingly. The therapist expects to be there Tuesday at five o'clock. The patient will come to the appointment doubting that next Tuesday will even appear on his horizon, but he will be pulled along by the anticipatory feeling of the future represented on the card. The nonschizophrenic person can plan for tomorrow; he can even take action today to meet the needs of the future. He buys life insurance, plans vacations, works today for pay in the future. He knows full well that the anticipated future may be changed by his death or some other circumstance. Nevertheless, he plans for the future knowing that the future will probably come. He has enough faith to conduct his life accordingly. But the schizophrenic person cannot make that leap of faith. He is immobilized in the present. The anticipatory pull into his future does not influence the experience of the present moment.

How much the anticipatory pull of the future is a part of life becomes clear when you imagine how your anticipation of the next few hours alters your experience at the moment when you are reading this. If you expect to spend a pleasant evening in pleasant company in pleasant surroundings, the experiences you have right now reading this section will be colored by that anticipation. You will enjoy, even now, knowing what is ahead. If, on the other hand, you anticipate a disastrous meeting with unpleasant people, leading to major changes in your life, then probably the present moment of reading is an unpleasant experience, you will have a hard time paying attention to this material, you will not be enjoying yourself, and your moment of reading will be disturbed by anxiety. The future is as important and active an influence on the present as is the past. The flow from past to present and from future to present is part of the experience of life for most of us. This flow is absent in the schizophrenic human being's experience of existence.

One of the major difficulties resulting in symptoms in the schizophrenic life is the failure to differentiate between what has occurred and what was only dreamed, fantasized, thought, hallucinated, or planned. Since personal experience is not readily available to recall, the consensually validated reality that is part of that experience is also absent.

Just as the problem with historicity influences the two other nuclear clusters of disability, those of anxiety management and interpersonal disasters, so also do they influence the failure of historicity. When the patient experiences much anxiety, this anxiety interferes with the incorporation of life's experiences. Similarly, when interpersonal misadventures result in pain and failure, they are less available for incorporation into the personal lived history. However, these observations do not explain the problem with historicity. We have no adequate explanation for this observed phenomenon. Perhaps eventually the failure of historicity will be attributed to a biochemical or anatomical or social learning defect. At the moment, we can only say that the failure of historicity, leading to the cluster of dysfunctions we have described, qualitatively and quantitatively distinguishes the lives of schizophrenic persons from that of nonschizophrenic persons.

Chapter 6

※※※※※※※※

Making the Diagnosis

Much has been written about the diagnosis of schizophrenia. There are those who propose that the diagnosis be so widely applied that the word *schizophrenia* becomes synonymous with all psychotic illnesses. Other authors choose to make the diagnostic category tight and to respond to their own frustrating experience of low inter-diagnostician reliability by requiring the presence of end-stage symptoms. Neither of these extreme positions is of much help in understanding, managing, treating, and prognosticating for the individual patient. If we insist that the diagnosis of schizophrenia can only be made when the patient has delusions, hallucinations, and grossly

49

disorganized behavior, then we are choosing to diagnose schizophrenia only at the end of a lifelong disability. At such a stage, diagnosis has little to offer.

The movement in medicine and in psychiatry that has confused civil rights and political liberalism with the practice of scientific medicine was a response to the misuse of diagnostic categories by society, by the government, by political groups, and by medicine itself. An antidiagnostic movement has arisen in psychiatry that has seriously influenced some of our younger colleagues to oppose the idea of diagnosing anyone in the field of mental health. Labeling human beings with this or that diagnosis may have serious negative consequences socially, politically, and economically for the individual. However, that problem cannot be solved by failing to make a diagnosis. It can only be solved by meticulously maintaining confidentiality of medical records and of the doctor-patient relationship. Diagnosis is a medical procedure that has medical meaning and that is of no value outside the medical system. (There have even been clinicians who have dealt with these serious social, economic, and political problems not only by refusing to make diagnosis but also by deliberately making the incorrect diagnosis. These acts have had the consequence that a lot of the current data available on hospital charts and in outpatient clinics is of no value for research.) To say that diagnoses should not be made because they have been misused and misapplied is nonsense. To say that diagnoses should not be made because they are difficult to make, and because our diagnostic techniques are not always as good as we want them to be, is also nonsense. To reserve diagnosis for terminal cases where the diagnosis is of little value is depriving ourselves of the usefulness that diagnostic categories have had in the history of medicine. To sharpen our approach to diagnosis, to train better diagnosticians, and to more clearly define the diagnostic categories is an appropriate response to the low interdiagnostician reliability found for the category of schizophrenia.

We are strongly in favor of making careful and correct diagnoses in psychiatry, as in all of medicine. A valid diagnosis carefully made, showing a high degree of interdiagnostician reliability, allows for planning treatment, estimation of prognosis, doing research, and understanding clinical problems within the framework of epidemiology studies.

The history of schizophrenia shows that the major symptom clusters were thought to be separate illnesses until Kraepelin recognized the relationship of hebephrenia, paranoia, and catatonia under the general heading of *dementia praecox*.

It became apparent during and after World War II that schizophrenic patients with multiple hospital admissions frequently carried a variety of diagnoses. On one occasion, someone would be seen as a paranoid schizophrenic. During subsequent hospitalizations, he would be diagnosed as catatonic schizophrenic, acute schizophrenic, chronic undifferentiated schizophrenic, simple schizophrenic, hebephrenic schizophrenic, and so on. It became apparent from these long-term records, available from the Veterans Administration and state hospital systems, that the same patient, having the same constellation of symptoms, would be called something different depending on what his major presenting problem was at the moment of examination. This variability led to the idea in the 1960s that various signs and symptoms predominating at various times in the individual's life were the result of his life circumstances and his psychological processes of the moment.

Symptom choice in part is also determined by the culture from which the patient comes, the social class in which he lives, and the specific circumstance in which he finds himself. In patients who have been ill for many years, the content of their paranoid delusions frequently is related to the major political, economic, or social concerns at the time of the onset of the illness. Patients who had been at a hospital for fifty or sixty years would have delusions about the Kaiser; patients who came somewhat later would talk about the Communists; then there was a group of patients who had delusional systems about the Nazis, and then came those who thought Senator McCarthy was after them. Their illnesses were not different but the content of their paranoia was related to the concern of the day at the time of their illness. Today, in the post-Watergate era, paranoid patients believe their phones are tapped and that tapes are being made about them. To talk about each of these systems as a separate illness makes as little sense as the French classification of the 1860s when each phobia was thought to be an entirely different illness.

Careful observation of the natural history of schizophrenia shows us that perhaps we have lumped too many conditions together in our eagerness to understand the pattern of illness. There is considerable evidence that several of the subtypes of schizophrenia have such a different natural history and such a different outcome and involve such an entirely different type of population that there may be justification to think of them as separate diseases. Questions were raised as we kept better records of the chronically mentally ill. Detailed studies and long-term follow-ups of schizophrenic patients have shown that a number of clusters of symptoms exist that have quite different outcomes and result in very different life histories for the patients. At the time of this writing, it seems useful to recognize three major groups of symptoms that traditionally have been called *schizophrenia* and that may be quite unrelated to each other.

The first of these symptom groups is childhood schizophrenia. The work of Loretta Bender and Leo Kanner (see Bakwin and Bakwin, 1972) has shown that the schizophrenic child (sometimes called the *autistic child*) is quite different from the schizophrenic adult. Even when the schizophrenic child becomes an adult, his residual childhood schizophrenia does not manifest itself like the usual adult schizophrenia. In the clinical course of childhood schizophrenia there is evidence of organicity, the course of the illness is quite different and the time of onset is much earlier than in the usual adult syndrome. It may indeed be a great disservice to our understanding of both children and adults to talk about this condition as *childhood schizophrenia,* since it has no real relationship to the condition which we call *schizophrenia* in adulthood.

Acute psychoses have been called *acute schizophrenic episodes.* These acute episodes can occur in chronic schizophrenic patients but also occur in many people whose history does not show schizophrenic illness or the schizophrenic life. These acute psychotic episodes can frequently only be diagnosed in retrospect as belonging to a schizophrenic illness when there is a history of two or three such episodes over a period of many years of chronic schizophrenic disability. It is generally impossible to make the diagnosis of schizophrenia on the basis of a mental status examination alone. In the acute episode there are major affective components, confusional states, disruption of reality testing, gross thought disorder, and behavioral abnormalities. The prognosis of these acute psychotic episodes is quite different from that for other schizophrenic episodes. The best studies indicate that 65 to 70 percent of these patients show spontaneous remission from the acute episodes. Studies also indicate that parents and siblings of patients having only one such acute episode show no higher incidence of schizophrenia than the general population. There is considerable difficulty in making the diagnosis of acute schizophrenia for the first and only episode even by well-trained diagnosticians. The confusion between acute schizophrenic episodes, acute organic states, acute toxic states, acute affective disorders, and schizoaffective disorders is great. Patients in these acute episodes respond well to all forms of treatment. This response is understandable, since two thirds of them seem to get well regardless of what is done. Only a small number of these patients develop a course that is similar to the category of chronic schizophrenia.

The third group of symptoms that has been called *schizophrenia* is the clinical syndrome of chronic schizophrenia. We propose that this group is the only category that should be called *schizophrenia;* that, in fact, schizophrenia by definition is a chronic illness, a chronic cluster of disabilities with a predictable course, a known natural history, and a response to treatment and nontreatment in predictable ways. We propose that the condition that has been called *childhood schizophrenia* and that the condition known as *acute schizophrenia* be removed from the diagnostic category of schizophrenia. The category of schizophrenia must be reserved for what traditionally has been called *chronic schizophrenia.* The chronic schizophrenic patients have a distinct and predictable clinical course and response to treatment.

In this category of schizophrenia, which we believe is the only one that belongs in this diagnostic classification, there are three subtypes. These subtypes are (1) paranoid schizophrenia, (2) chronic intermittent schizophrenia, and (3) chronic latent schizophrenia. In the next chapter, the prognosis and natural history of these illnesses will be discussed in detail, showing the differences in the course of lives afflicted by such difficulties.

Aside from paranoid symptoms, paranoid schizophrenia shows the three nuclear disabilities of management of anxiety; impaired, clumsy, and disastrously ending interpersonal relationships; and the major failure of historicity. However, this particular type of schizophrenia shows very little evidence of some of the secondary difficulties that have been described by Bleuler, Schneider, or the Washington University group (Robins and Guze, 1970).

The second subtype of schizophrenia, the chronic intermittent type, is one that has characteristically been diagnosed as chronic schizophrenia. These patients have a lifelong course of illness with prolonged periods in which major psychotic symptoms are absent, interspersed with periods of acute exacerbation. They show varying patterns of symptoms at various times in their lives. In the past they have been diagnosed as schizoaffective, hebephrenic, simple, catatonic, and so on. Their acute exacerbations may be misdiagnosed as acute schizophrenic episodes, and during remissions they look so much like latent schizophrenic patients that they may be misdiagnosed as having character disorders or neuroses. However, these chronic intermittent schizophrenic patients clearly show the triad of the three nuclear clusters of disabilities that we propose as pathognomonic of schizophrenia. The careful clinician and skilled observer can find the three disabilities even during the periods when the patient is grossly asymptomatic.

Traditionally, a diagnosis of schizoaffective schizophrenia has been included in the group of schizophrenias. These patients seem to have many of the symptoms of schizophrenia, but they also tend to have more of an affective component to their symptomatology. Whether such a separate diagnostic category exists has been the basis of argument in psychiatry for the past thirty years. It seems to us that the most rational position is presented by the Washington University group as exemplified in the work of Eli Robins and others, which essentially concludes that schizoaffective psychosis is a diagnosis representing a mixed clinical picture but not a separate illness. Schizoaffective psychosis includes patients who two years later look clearly schizophrenic but who at the time of initial examination had major affective components in their psychotic episodes. It also includes patients who clearly belong in the group of affective psychosis but who show some major schizophrenialike symptoms. Two years later those patients who are now on occasion classified as schizoaffective either look clearly schizophrenic or seem to belong to the affective group. Schizophrenic patients can show affective symptoms such as depression and manic excitement during the acute episode without being removed from the category of schizophrenic illnesses.

The third subtype of schizophrenia, latent schizophrenia, has in the past been called *pseudoneurotic schizophrenia, residual schizophrenia,* and so on. Such a person has the cluster of the three nuclear disabilities but at no time in his life shows the gross psychotic symptoms. In every other way, he is like the chronic intermittent schizophrenic, except that he has no intermittent psychotic episodes. Yet, even though such patients are frequently misdiagnosed as neurotic because of the absence of acute psychotic symptoms, they are clearly different from neurotic patients and they clearly show the lifelong problems that we see as characteristic of schizophrenia. Robert Knight (1953) and others have proposed that this group of patients, whom he calls the *borderline patients,* can sometimes be diagnosed only if they are treated as though they were neurotic, which treatment then produces the more severe symptoms leading to disorganization. If one does a free-associative interview or engages in analytic, insight, nonstructured psychotherapy, the latent schizo- phrenic patient may disorganize and show major symptoms of psychosis. Engaging the patient in the ambiguous, ill-defined situa- tion of the psychoanalytic psychotherapy situation produces a stress that magnifies the basic defects and lays bare the underlying schizo- phrenic organization. Such a procedure may be likened to a glucose tolerance test, which will demonstrate sugar metabolism difficulties under the stress of glucose ingestion even though blood sugar after fasting may be normal.

Eugen Bleuler (1950) proposed that four fundamental symptoms of schizophrenia were present in every case and had to be described in order to make the diagnosis. These four symptoms are disturbances of association, affective indifference and inappropriate- ness, autism, and ambivalence. Medical students and psychiatrists have recited these four pathognomonic symptoms as characteristic of schizophrenia for almost 100 years. Yet when these symptoms are applied to the individual case, major difficulties arise. For ex- ample, the disturbances of association, or loose associations, which are manifested by the tangentiality and rambling and peculiar logic such patients express, are seen under conditions of severe anxiety even in normal subjects. It appears that the loose associations that have traditionally been described as part of the picture of schizophrenia are a secondary result of a high level of free-floating anxiety. It is true that under "normal" conditions schizophrenic patients show loose associations, while nonschizophrenic people do not. This tendency is a manifestation of the inability of schizophrenics to manage anxiety.

The affective indifference and inappropriateness that Bleuler thought was characteristic of schizophrenic patients turns out in fact not to be true. It is quite possible to observe affective indifference and inappropriateness if one spends only a few moments with a patient. However, when the examiner gets to know a patient well, it becomes clear that the schizophrenic patient, rather than showing affective flatness or indifference, shows a mercurial, labile, and changable affect. As part of his withdrawal he withholds affective response in the social contact. What has been described as inappropriate affect turns out to be very appropriate to his own private thoughts when we know the patient. It is, however, socially inappropriate and frequently appears inappropriate to consensually validated reality. I have never seen a schizophrenic patient whose affect was inappropriate to his own thought processes.

The third symptom—autism—leads to diagnostic problems. As a group, schizophrenic patients tend to be less in contact with external reality and more in touch with their own personal, idiosyncratic reality. The same condition of paying more attention to what is inside than what is outside can be observed in a large variety of states in the range of religious preoccupation, creativity, meditation, hearing loss, and language difficulty. Such normal preoccupation with the inner life and withdrawal from the environment is on occasion difficult to distinguish from the autism of schizophrenia in the individual person.

Ambivalence is the most difficult symptom to apply. As each one of us can be ambivalent about everything, ambivalence is part of the human condition. The difference between the ambivalence of the schizophrenic person and the ambivalence of the nonschizophrenic person is not the quantity or quality of ambivalence but in the effect the ambivalence has on behavior. Generally, the schizophrenic person is immobilized by his ambivalence, while others can resolve it.

Bleuler (1950) thought that all other symptoms are accessory and may or may not be present at a given time in a schizophrenia case. We feel that even his fundamental symptoms are not present in every case. (We have discussed in considerable detail the relationship of Bleuler's fundamental and accessory symptoms to the three nuclear disabilities in the preceding chapters.)

The diagnostic and statistical manual of the American Psychiatric Association (APA) focuses on the difficulty in schizophrenia of disturbances of thinking, mood, and behavior. Although this approach is useful in severe and terminal cases and does differentiate schizophrenias from the affective disorders, it often does not help much in the diagnosis of the individual case. The disturbances of thinking in the paranoid schizophrenic patient are very limited and may not show the disturbances of association or idiosyncratic logic beyond the one small area that is included in the paranoid system. In the latent schizophrenic patient, disturbances of thinking may not be present at any time. We have already discussed in the preceding paragraphs the difficulty in using the disturbances of mood and disturbances of behavior as diagnostic signs. These signs are nonspecific in the schizophrenic person and they appear as major symptoms only in the end state of the psychotic episode.

The Washington University group (Robins and Guze, 1970) has attempted to refine the application of diagnostic criteria. They, too, insist that we are dealing with the chronic illness and they propose that symptoms must exist for at least 6 months before a diagnosis of schizophrenia can be made. However, the symptoms they insist on are not the nuclear disabilities that we have elaborated, but rather the end symptoms of schizophrenia. They require delusions or hallucinations or difficulty in communication and thinking for the diagnosis of schizophrenia. They also propose the absence of depressive or manic symptoms severe enough to place the patient in the category of affective psychoses. They include evidence of poor social adjustment, a family history of schizophrenia, onset of illness prior to age forty, and the absence of alcohol and drug abuse prior to the onset of psychosis. Although the approach of Feighner and of the Washington group does much to refine the concept of schizophrenia, these criteria are not very helpful to the individual clinician facing the individual patient and having to make a diagnosis.

Kurt Schneider (1959) has proposed eleven first-rank symptoms of schizophrenia that he feels are helpful in defining the diagnostic category of the schizophrenic patient (see Chapter 2). It is clear from reviewing these first-rank symptoms that when the patient shows these he is in an end state of the illness. Since the purpose of diagnosis is to allow for early and correct treatment intervention and for prognostication of outcome, if we insist on Schneider's first-rank symptoms we will be making the diagnosis of schizophrenia retrospectively. We will be able to say that this patient is clearly schizophrenic only at that point when there is not much value to making the diagnosis, for at that point we will be able to say that the patient has been schizophrenic for five, ten, or twenty years. Schneider's first-rank symptoms are in fact secondary complications of badly managed or untreated cases of schizophrenia. Schneider's first-rank symptoms are restitutive attempts to deal with the nuclear disabilities of schizophrenia. There is considerable recent evidence to show that these restitutive symptoms are seriously influenced by cultural and language background.

We must say the same about other attempts to systematize the diagnostic category of schizophrenic by classifying the appearance of end symptoms. Yusin and his associates (1974) examined records of admission to the Los Angeles County-University of Southern California (LAC-USC) Medical Center of psychotic patients and then tabulated the frequency of symptoms. He discovered that schizophrenic patients had delusions and hallucinations and therefore proposed that these are primary symptoms of schizophrenia. He tabulated the end state of an illness in the special population of schizophrenic patients who were admitted to the LAC-USC Medical Center. This special population consisted of schizophrenic patients whose homeostasis had been upset and whose end symptoms were the result of a devastating life history including severe psychological symptoms, economic problems, social and political disenfranchisement, and so forth.

We propose that the diagnosis of schizophrenia in the life of an individual must be made early enough to be of value in planning a treatment program and to offer prognostic guidelines. Since the treatment of schizophrenia is entirely different from the treatment of neurosis and the major affective disorders, it is crucial that we develop an approach that allows adequate accuracy of diagnosis and clear differentiation of schizophrenia from other mental illness. And since the signs and symptoms proposed by Kraepelin, Bleuler, Schneider, and others are the secondary restitutive responses of the person to the three nuclear disabilities and since these symptoms are found in the end states of the illness, we propose that the diagnosis be based on the detection of three nuclear disabilities. The first is the disability of anxiety management, characterized by failure to manage and bind anxiety with the exhaustion of psychological energy in the attempt. The second disability is the clumsiness and disastrous outcome of interpersonal relationships. The third disability is the failure of historicity. Each of these requires taking a careful history and implies the presence of these difficulties over a prolonged time. We insist on chronicity in our definition of schizophrenia. We do not propose to give a standard formula for the length of time the symptoms have to be present. The Washington University group stipulated six months. In our experience there is nothing magical about six months. We feel that the diagnosis can be made when a picture emerges that shows, from a carefully taken history, that the pattern of disabilities is consistent. Each of these disabilities can exist in many people who are not schizophrenic at any one moment. Who has not had periods when he was unable to manage his anxiety adequately and showed some disorganization of function? Who has not experienced neurasthenia or exhaustion from carrying high levels of anxiety and attempting to cope for several days? What human being who lives life has not had problems in the area of interpersonal relationships? Certainly each of us has been clumsy at times in our dealing with our fellow man. There are periods in each of our lives where our own personal lived history seems not to be available to us to draw on as a base of experience from which to alter our behavior and our judgments. Yet only in schizophrenia are all three of these disabilities present at the same time over an extended period. When we see the human being who cannot manage his anxiety and who is exhausted in the effort, who enters into each human relationship clumsily and unsuccessfully, and comes away from each relationship feeling worse about himself,

FIGURE 1. CLASSIFICATION OF SCHIZOPHRENIA SUBTYPES

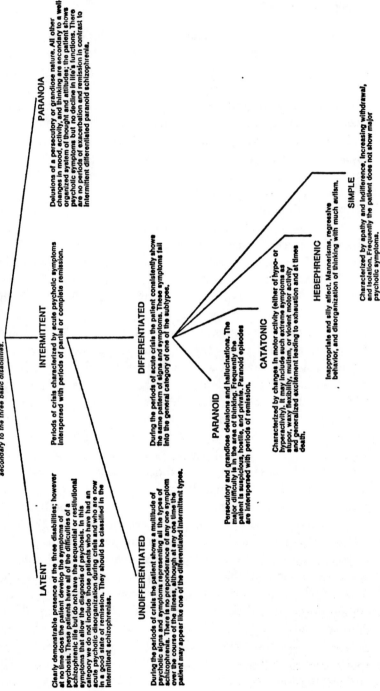

who faces each day as though it were the first day of his life, then we can make the diagnosis of schizophrenia. Making the diagnosis on this basis allows us to do it early enough to be of value, with enough certainty and reliability to be within usual medical standards, and specifically enough not to include in the diagnostic category all sorts of other conditions that have a very different natural history and prognosis.

Chapter 7

⋇⋇⋇⋇⋇⋇⋇⋇

Natural History and Prognosis

In order to assess the efficacy of the treatment intervention in a chronic illness such as schizophrenia, it is absolutely essential that we have a clear idea of the natural history of the illness in its untreated form. We must understand what the lives of human beings are like who are afflicted by schizophrenia and what the course of their difficulties is like. The literature on schizophrenia over the past several centuries describes a great multitude of treatment interventions that have been reported as beneficial. However, since there has been so much confusion about diagnosis that many conditions have been included in this diagnostic category, treatment is difficult to evaluate. Evaluation proved to be even more complicated after we learned that much of what was thought to be the outcome of schizophrenic illness turned out to be results of treatment. Because in the latter part of the nineteenth century and the first part of the twentieth century schizophrenic persons were chronically hospitalized, they developed the consequences of such chronic hospitalization.

One of the observations we have been able to make over the past three decades is that if the patient is not treated with techniques that cause physical damage to his nervous system, or social and psychological damage to his person, then the course of illness does not lead to mental deterioration. Therefore, our ideas about prognosis have changed.

To be consistent (see Chapter 6), when we talk about the prognosis in schizophrenia and the natural history of this illness, we are excluding those conditions that lead to an unstable diagnostic category. We exclude those acute psychotic episodes that do not lead to a chronic course. We are excluding schizoaffective illnesses until we have a two-year history in which the patient appears to fit clearly into the schizophrenic diagnostic category. We also exclude childhood schizophrenia.

Even if we limit ourselves to the more precise diagnostic category of schizophrenia—defining it as an illness that is chronic and that has periods of remission and exacerbation, and limiting it to an illness characterized by the three nuclear disabilities of problems in anxiety management, interpersonal relationship, and failure of historicity—we still have a considerable difference of opinion among various researchers and research centers as to the prognosis of schizophrenia. Improved precision in the diagnosis of schizophrenia based on the natural history approach will allow us to say more useful things about the prognosis in schizophrenia.

It was discovered during the first half of this century that there was a group of schizophrenic patients who had a good prognosis and there seemed to be another group of schizophrenic patients who had a poor prognosis. In these studies, patients included in the schizophrenic diagnostic category varied from place to place. If the diagnosis of schizophrenia was based on one acute psychotic episode, then we know that many patients will have an excellent prognosis and will have no further difficulty with the "schizophrenic" illness. We have concluded that in fact such patients frequently suffer from an entirely different condition, which has such a different course from schizophrenia that they should not be called *schizophrenic*. When patients who are diagnosed as having schizophrenia during the acute episode are studied over the following years, it becomes clear that a number of these are in fact suffering from affective psychosis or schizophreniform acute psychotic episodes.

The ideas about prognosis have been changing. Everyone who is concerned with schizophrenia attempts to clarify prognosis either for the evaluation of treatment or to provide economical interventions. In general, the outcome of schizophrenia is quite similar to the outcome of other illnesses—25 percent of patients seem to improve regardless of what treatment techniques are used or if indeed no treatment is used. Another 25 percent seem not to improve significantly no matter what treatment method is used, and 50 percent of the patient population seem to get better if treated and seem not to improve if not treated. It becomes important to identify the group of patients for whom limited and expensive treatment resources should be used, because treatment might make a difference in the life course of such patients. In an attempt to identify the group of patients in whom treatment makes a difference, much has been written about the good-prognosis, as opposed to poor-prognosis schizophrenic patients. Depending on what part of the world the studies come from, good prognosis versus bad prognosis has also been called *process* versus *reactive schizophrenia, schizophrenia* versus *schizophreniform illness,* and so on. Attempts to differentiate patients have been sought in terms of a difference in the course of the illness. In the 1940s the studies tended to focus on premorbid personality (Polatin and Hoch, 1947). The patient's condition before the index acute psychotic episode determined prognosis. The clinician predicted good prognosis both for remission from the acute psychotic episode and for long-term follow-up (predicting the number and severity of future exacerbations and the quality and length of remissions between these exacerbations) on the basis of how the patient was before he became acutely ill this time. If the precipitating stress was clearly identifiable; if the onset was sudden; if the patient functioned well before the acute exacerbation of illness; if he had been able to establish some relationship with people (getting married, having friends); if he had been able to manage his anxiety well enough to function at work or at home; if he had been able to function socially—then his prognosis would be good. If the onset were insidious; if the symptoms were slowly emerging (not particularly showing confusion or stunnedness); if he had been unable to function in a social or economic or intellectual way even before the acute exacerbation; if he had not been able to establish any relationship and had lived an isolated and alienated existence; if there were no clearly identifiable precipitating stress— then his prognosis would be poor. Subsequent studies have attempted to elaborate on this description and to relate prognosis to type of schizophrenic illness. A number of scales have even been developed to classify premorbid adjustment into good prognosis and poor prognosis. Retrospective studies to identify the major predictive factors have been attempted. The outcome is circular. Studies indicate that chronicity predicts chronicity, that poor function predicts poor prognosis. We have come back to a conclusion very similar to the findings of the studies of the 1940s. It appears now that a total evaluation of the life of an individual who has schizophrenia makes sense only if we also look at what else he has besides his schizophrenia. We must not only look at premorbid personality but also look at the total picture of the individual, the world in which he lives, the coping demands made on him, and the world he creates for himself. We must evaluate his abilities as well as his disabilities, his assets as well as his liabilities.

Perhaps we can clarify the scope of evaluation if we look at the natural history of a human being in his life. We know that the individual is born in a physiologically and psychologically helpless position. He needs to be nurtured and taken care of until he develops independence. As he grows up and moves toward independence, he faces certain crises that are a part of every human existence. These are crises of change, of adjustment, of increasing complexity of personal life. He then frequently takes on caring for others, whether they be his children, or friends, or patients. Psychoanalysts have described maturity as the ability to deal with dependency needs by taking care of others. The individual ages, his physical as well as psychological world changes, new demands are made on him for adaptation, his psychosocial space shrinks. Frequently the aged person needs increasing care and has to be dependent on others. The normal life cycle of each human being changes from dependence to independence and then perhaps back to dependence again. We change from being taken care of, to taking care of ourselves, to caring for others, and finally to being taken care of again. We move from a simple environment, to a more complex environment, to a highly complex situation, to a more simplified one, and then sometimes back to a very simple one. The entire life of the individual consists of changing, adapting, and coping. In the really healthy individual, there may be more than coping; there may be a zest for change, particularly at those times in his life when he feels confident and competent, when he feels in charge of his own existence.

The times in which all people face stress can be identified and can be correlated with periods of life in which there is more dysfunction, more social, psychological, and physical disorganization. In these periods we observe a more frequent onset of mental and emotional illness. Adolescence is the first of these periods. There is a disparate rate of physical, social, psychological, economic, and interpersonal growth. It is a time of storm and stress for each human being, a time when individuals with fewer coping abilities tend to flounder. The next period of stress is seen when we complicate our existences by entering into intimate relationships that involve commitment and concern, relationships that are expressed in closeness, love, and marriage. Next comes the stress when we take on the role of responsibility of caring for others. This stress may be signaled by a time of having children, or by a period of graduation, becoming a person who is fully trained and competent. The next stress in human existence frequently is related to periods in middle life when the individual begins to ask questions about the meaning of his existence. He wonders whether what he has, what he is doing, what he is striving for, is in fact what he is willing to settle for. The individual faces such questions as "Is that all there is to it?" "Is that all it is about?" This stress period is frequently related to external signals of having arrived at whatever goals were set. The next stress in human existence is when the decline begins. This period may be signaled by retirement, by menopause, by the children moving out of the house, by declining income, by declining physical ability, by facing declining physical functions, or by the appearance of chronic illness. Finally comes the difficult task of growing old gracefully. Aged people face the problem of increasing dependence, of accepting limitations, and of facing changes leading to termination rather than beginnings.

One may say that each of these points of stress is a progressive closing of the future. It is a point at which the human existence moves from "All is possible," to "Some things are possible," to "It may be possible," to "It might have been possible," and finally to "It will never be." Human beings have invented social customs and traditions that help with these difficult transitional stages. Many of these traditions are embedded in religion, in the culture, and the social customs such as for marriage, birth, death, and mourning. Yet these points of transition are difficult for everyone. Human beings handle them with the assets they have available for coping. When coping devices do not suffice, then transitory dysfunctions appear that may take the form of depression, temporary disorganization of function, or neuroses. These periods of transition are the boulders in the path of life over which each of us has to climb. These boulders in the part of the life of schizophrenic individuals seem insurmountable. Since the schizophrenic person does not just stumble over the boulders, but stumbles even over pebbles of everyday existence, it becomes clear that these transition points are frequently a source of dysfunction.

In the natural history of schizophrenic illness, the onset of the first clinical symptom is often during adolescence. We have noted that acute exacerbations appear when the schizophrenic individual enters into demanding, close, intimate relationships, such as getting married. We have noted that many schizophrenic persons develop acute exacerbation during postpartum stages for the woman and for the man when the child becomes a complicating factor in the psychosocial space of the family. Human beings who suffer from schizophrenia do particularly poorly when changes are required of them. Demands of adaptation in middle life and late life are poorly handled and frequently result in acute exacerbation of psychotic symptoms interrupting what seems like a fairly good remission.

When we attempt the task of predicting which patient will

do well or poorly, we must look at what else the individual has besides schizophrenia. It is not the illness that predicts the prognosis; it is the total human being who predicts the prognosis. If someone is bright, beautiful, talented, rich, educated, part of a society that appreciates him, and comes from a family and an environment that offers much support, then he has a good prognosis for life. If the same individual also has schizophrenia, then he has a good prognosis for living with his schizophrenia. But if the individual comes from a deprived background in which little support is offered, in which social skills and social customs were not learned, if he is also poor and disenfranchised; if he is stupid and ugly; if he lives in a culture or in a society that finds him repulsive—then his prognosis for living a good life is poor. If he also has schizophrenia, then his prognosis for having a good course of schizophrenia is poor. We must not ask what the difference between good prognosis and poor prognosis in schizophrenia is, but rather we must ask what the difference between good prognosis and poor prognosis for life is. The prognosis for schizophrenia is the same as the prognosis for life.

Frequently clinicians become circular in their reasoning about prognosis, confusing cause and effect in terms of premorbid personality. Some clinicians observe that an individual who is married has a better prognosis than an individual who has never been married. Therefore, they conclude that marriage leads to good prognosis in schizophrenia. The capacities that allow an individual to enter into a marriage relationship with a fellow human being are precisely the same capacities that allow him to handle his schizophrenia effectively. The individual who does not have enough assets and social skills to interest any other human being to spend time with him on a commitment such as marriage has great difficulty handling his schizophrenia.

The course of the illness of the chronic patient who has more generalized disorganization, with poorer quality of remission, is worse than the patient who has better remissions and shorter psychotic episodes. Clinical observation reveals that the more severe the symptoms of the acute episode, the better the prognosis is for a good remission of that acute episode. Of the chronic, intermittent, differentiated schizophrenias, certain clusters of symptoms are associated with a poorer prognosis. The catatonic symptoms tend to be associated with the better prognosis, while the paranoid and hebephrenic clusters of symptoms are associated with poorer prognosis.

In summary, then, the natural history of the human being who has schizophrenia is very similar to the natural history of the human being who does not have schizophrenia. He faces the same problems in living and the same need for adaptation. The difference is that he has an impaired capacity in dealing with these problems and needs, that his response pattern to these stresses is more disorganized and leads to the clinical picture of mental illness. People who have a better prognosis for life are individuals who have more coping assets, which lead to increased flexibility and increased adaptational capacities. People who have a poor prognosis for life lack these capacities. If they also have schizophrenia, their prognosis for living with schizophrenia parallels their prognosis for life.

Chapter 8

⋙⋙⋙⋘⋘⋘

Genetic Theories　　　　*Robert E. Allen*

At the present time, there is little doubt that schizophrenia is a genetically determined disorder. The nature-nurture, heredity-environment controversies of the past are now of only historic importance. The either/or notion of heredity and environment, which consumed energy hardly commensurate with true gain, has been replaced by the more accurate but sometimes misleading notion that the truth is to be found in the interface between genetics and environment. A problem in determining the etiology of a psychological disease is the tendency to assume that such a disease is caused by psychological factors. Although the environment may allow the genotype to express itself clinically, that environment may be biochemical rather than psychological.

Part of the difficulty in genetic research in schizophrenia is the lack of easily identifiable biochemical markers, such as those found in phenylketonuria or diabetes. Other difficulties have to do with the problems of diagnosis that confound both biochemical and genetic research. In spite of these difficulties, the question now is not one of genetic determination, but how and why it occurs.

It is not the intent of this chapter to summarize genetic studies in the field. Excellent review articles have been recently published by Heston (1973) and Shields (1968), which do not need to be replicated here. Genetic studies have fallen into three categories: the older studies of concordance in twins, the compilations of incidence in families, and the newer and more definitive studies of the offspring of schizophrenic individuals.

Kallmann's famous series, which gave initial impetus to establishing genetic factors in the etiology of schizophrenia, yielded a concordance now considered to be quite a bit too high (Kallmann, 1938). His nearly 86 percent monozygotic concordance was probably caused by the overdiagnosis of schizophrenia, by problems with age correction factors, and by the fact that his cases were selected from a chronic hospital population and thus may have been biased toward severe cases. Although it has been established that the more severe the disease in the proband, the greater the likelihood for concordance in the twin, this correlation is probably not enough to explain his high rates. On the other hand, Tienari's monozygotic concordance of 0 percent also suffers from diagnostic problems and the young age of his subjects at time of study (Tienari, 1968). Even so, concordance in the major studies since World War II falls halfway between Kallmann's high and Tienari's low and is generally assumed to be 40 to 45 percent. In addition, probably another 40 to 45 percent of the co-twins, while not schizophrenic, are significantly impaired psychiatrically. Thus, only 10 to 20 percent of monozygotic co-twins are normal, while 80 to 90 percent are either schizophrenic or fall in the genetic schizophrenic spectrum.

The fact that 100 percent concordance is not found in monozygotic twins is often used by those arguing against genetic implication, another either/or concept that is not consistent with current thinking about genetics. An example can be found in medicine. The concordance for diabetes mellitus is approximately 40 to 45 percent in monozygotic twins. Since we have better biochemical techniques for identifying this disease than for schizophrenia, it is possible to find the genotype in 100 percent of those twins, 10 percent of them having abnormal glucose tolerance curves, and the other 45 percent having an abnormal plasma insulin response to infused glucose. Diabetes, a disease that is assuredly genetically determined, is influenced to a significant degree by environment in terms of obesity and diet. Its mild and severe forms, while sharing some clinical similarities, are quite different in terms of clinical course, response to treatment, and age of onset. Indeed, if we possessed a sophisticated enough means of identification, we might be able to find the schizophrenic genotype in 100 percent of all monozygotic twins. Such devices still do not answer the question of why the genotype is expressed in only some individuals.

Studies of the nontwin relatives of schizophrenic persons also show a strong evidence for genetic factors (Shields, 1968). The risk for one who is the sibling of a schizophrenic person with neither parent schizophrenic is about 8 percent; with one parent schizophrenic, about 12 percent; and with both parents schizophrenic, around 35 percent. Although early estimates of incidence in dizygotic twins were about 15 percent, later estimates seem to be closer to the 8 to 9 percent estimated in nontwin siblings. Although we might assume that the chaotic environment in the family of a schizophrenic person might be an important etiological factor, it has been demonstrated that probably about 70 percent of the nonpsychotic children of two schizophrenic parents are relatively normal. Studies of several generations have been compiled by Karlsson (1972), who, for example, traces the genealogy of the children of an Icelandic farmer and his wife, both born in 1682. He finds that schizophrenia shows a familial continuity through seven generations, segregating into high-rate families or families with the general population rate.

However significant the evidence from twin and family studies that schizophrenia was a genetic disease, much criticism focused on the impossibility of sorting out the effects of environment in children exposed to the same rearing practices. Heston (1966) showed a significant change in experimental design in the first of many papers dealing with the adopted-away offspring of schizophrenic parents. The initial study dealt with a relatively small group of children adopted from schizophrenic mothers in a state hospital shortly after birth. Not only was there an incidence of schizophrenia much higher than that of the general population in these children, but the incidence of the schizoid or schizophrenic spectrum disorders was almost 50 percent in the children who were not schizophrenic. Of the several other studies dealing with the offspring of schizophrenics, the most definitive seem to be the recent Danish studies of Kety and others (in press), partly unpublished. Adopted children in Denmark who became schizophrenic served as the focus for comparison of their true or biologic family and their family and their adopted one. The fact that the biologic relatives of adopted schizophrenic persons showed a significant incidence of schizophrenia, roughly corresponding to the figures described in earlier studies for parents and siblings, seems to offer the definitive statement of genetic determination in the illness.

What does remain open to debate is the mode of genetic transmission. A dominant autosomal gene with incomplete penetrance, a polygenic mode, or even double-locus theories, all fit the empirical data at the present. Lately, with the introduction of modifying genes into the dominant model, the theories are beginning to merge. At present, there is no answer, but future research may offer one.

A major area occupying current thinking is the need to isolate factors that allow the genotype of schizophrenia to find its phenotypic expression. Although this research is in its early stages, both in conception and actual studies, there are exciting recent findings that implicate physical and biochemical rather than psychic stress. Mednick (1970), in his studies of children at risk for schizophrenia, found a more than threefold incidence of perinatal birth problems in those children who become schizophrenic, as compared to the children who do not. The Mednick study is still in its early phases, as the mean age of the children is in the early twenties, and much further work in the field needs to be done. The Genain quadruplets, while frequently used as examples of psychic determination of the severity of schizophrenia, could instead be different in their expression of the disease because of such biochemical factors.

Present and future research in the genetics of schizophrenia must deal with the question of the reason for the worldwide prevalence of the disease. Unless we explain it by a constant mutation of the specific gene, an explanation that seems unlikely in terms of genetic theories, there should be some positive value attached to the trait. A common model of the benefit of a genetically determined disease is that of sickle-cell anemia in which the disease is the malignant expression of a genotype (sickle-cell trait) that ameliorates malaria. If we search for advantages in relatives of schizophrenics who do not show the disease but who may be assumed to have some of the genotype, some highly intriguing findings arise that are not too different from the lay notion that schizophrenia is intelligence gone awry. Going back to Heston's original study (1966), we find that in those 50 percent of the adopted-away offspring of schizophrenic mothers who do not develop schizophrenia, there is a much-better-than-average life adjustment in terms of creativity and productivity. Admittedly, these fairly intangible factors are not entirely operationally definable. Karlsson's long-term genealogic studies in Iceland offer the observation that the families of schizophrenics show a more creative and more productive life as measured by "creativity quotient" (Karlsson, 1972). In addition, there seems to be a highly significant correlation between the 1944 *Who is Who in Iceland* and the registry of psychosis. Along somewhat different lines there is work indicating that relatives of schizophrenic persons are apparently less susceptible to viral infections (Carter and Watts, 1971).

Major thrusts of current research involve discovering the environmental factors, which may well be biochemical, and the intriguing question of the "purpose" of the genetic trait itself. With further advances in the biochemistry of schizophrenia, we will be better able to define the genetic trait and perhaps will reach a point in which we can determine the genotype in 100 percent of cases just as we can in diabetes. Kety (1976) has recently suggested the development of some system to continually monitor the fetal environment of children who will be at risk on birth. Although such an endeavor would be quite difficult, it is along these lines that an answer may be found. In terms of the usefulness of the trait, studies focusing on the schizophrenic person himself seem to show nothing that would select for the gene. However, studies of the relatives seem to lead to rather inescapable conclusions about the families in which schizophrenia is present.

Chapter 9

꙾꙾꙾꙾꙾꙾꙾꙾

Physical Theories

Robert E. Allen

The search for a specific physical defect in schizophrenia has long occupied those seeking the etiology of the disease. Based on models from medicine and reflecting current vogues, emphasis has shifted from the specific anatomic brain pathology sought at the turn of the century to the present attempts to identify a biochemical deficit or toxin. At present there is almost a surfeit of biochemical information and quite often there is a flurry of excitement about a newly discovered abnormality or toxic substance specific to schizophrenia. The usual subsequent history of such a discovery is either a failure to replicate initial results, or a series of reports finding the abnormality in a variety of normal and abnormal states. It is an assumption rather than definite fact that knowledge of the biochemistry of the major psychoses has become more specific and precise in past years. Although there is consensus that brain biochemistry and neurophysiology hold most if not all of the answers, the specific nature of the alteration has not yet been determined. Past research problems involving lack of attention to diagnosis, failure to correct for such factors as diet, and differences between acute and chronic schizophrenic persons are being corrected by the recognition that the problem is complex and by more sophisticated research designs.

The search for specific anatomic deficits in schizophrenia seems least promising as an area for future research. Probably derived from the general paresis model of mental illness and from the successful identification of the spirochete, the notion that pathological changes in the brain might be demonstrated in schizophrenia has held a strong attraction. Indeed, with the interest in dopamine and dopaminergic pathways, there have been attempts to map out the neural pathways of schizophrenia in much the same manner as we map out those pathways controlling pain or motor function. Thus, the nigrostraital system and the mesolimbic dopamine system are discussed as being possible neural pathways for schizophrenia. This notion seems a rather simplified explanation of complex neurophysiologic and neurochemical systems. Although there are mechanisms postulated involving neural pathways, cerebral blood flow, the autonomic nervous system, and other anatomic variables, there is no good evidence that any specific anatomic system is consistently altered in schizophrenia.

Physiologic changes have been studied with a variety of parameters. In spite of being contradictory and muddled by the lack of attention to precise diagnosis, there are some interesting descriptive trends. Physiologic studies (Payne, 1970) can apparently divide schizophrenic persons into high-arousal and low-arousal categories that show different clinical courses and different clusters of symptomatology, although little of an etiologic nature can be determined. There has also been an extensive search for abnormalities in electrophysiology as measured by electroencephalograms (EEG's) and evoked potentials. Recent work using computers and comparing different variables remains inconclusive. Although there are recent reports of abnormal EEG's in children at risk and many investigators have reported excess fast activity (Fink, 1973), there remain no characteristic EEG findings for schizophrenia. Evoked potentials have also been studied extensively, with no conclusive findings other than the apparent ability to distinguish male from female schizophrenic patients.

Biochemical theories of etiology of schizophrenia are changing rapidly. A few years ago, lysergic acid diethylamide (LSD) supplied the model for the toxic psychosis felt to most closely resemble schizophrenia. More recent evidence, both clinical and biochemical, indicates that a more pertinent model would be the amphetamine psychosis. Until recently, norepinephrine was the neurotransmitter most widely studied, but dopamine now seems to be assuming the central place in the postulated neurochemistry of schizophrenia. At present, notions of the biochemical etiology of schizophrenia can be grouped into two broad categories, the toxic metabolite/transmethylation theories and the abnormal protein theories.

More than twenty years ago, Harley-Mason (1952) first proposed that abnormally methylated biproducts of normal neural metabolites might be the psychotoxic source of schizophrenia. The exact nature of the toxic product was initially thought to resemble mescaline, which is structurally similar to norepinephrine and dopamine. The search for abnormalities in methylation has involved both catecholamines (dimethyoxy phenylethylamine [DMPEA], pink spot) and indoleamines (bufotenin). As with many biologic findings, results are equivocal, DMPEA (3-, 4-dimethoxy phenylethylamine) being a weak hallucinogen, and bufotenin probably not being hallucinogenic at all. DMPEA, however, does represent a methylated hallucinogen found frequently, if not consistently, in the urine of schizophrenic persons. Another frequent finding, consistent with the transmethylation hypothesis, is a worsening of symptoms in schizophrenic persons given methyl donors, such as methionine or betaine. It would have been even nicer for our theories if the treatment methodology of giving methyl acceptors, such as nicotinic acid or nicotinamide, indeed caused significant improvement in schizophrenic persons. But such treatment has not proved of significant value. Even so, there is a growing body of data, consistent with the broadest applications of the transmethylation hypothesis, which seems to be replicable by a variety of investigators.

At first glance, simple application of the toxic substance model fails to account for much that we know of the clinical course of schizophrenia. It seems difficult to fit such a model to a disease with late expression, exacerbation, and remissions. However, there could be a number of variables that we are not successfully able to conceptualize at present. It has been pointed out, for example, that if our diet were essentially lacking in phenylalanine, phenylketonuria could show a clinical course quite similar to that of schizophrenia. Recently, a model has been proposed by Stein and Wise (1971) that can account for the clinical course of schizophrenia and that also fits the currently fashionable dopaminergic system. Their model, which is supported by some experimental evidence in both animal and human studies, involves a deficiency in the enzyme that converts dopamine to norepinephrine. The resultant buildup of an aberrant by-product, 6-hydroxydopamine, is then postulated to have toxic destructive effects on a central nervous system (CNS) "reward" system. This model rather neatly explains differences in acute and chronic symptomatology and also accounts for drug efficacy by postulating that phenothiazines block the entry of the toxin into the nerve terminals.

Theories of abnormal proteins have been popular in biochemical research since Heath propounded taraxein in the 1950s. Although Heath's work (1958) has suffered greatly by failure of replication, many investigators have pursued his notions of protein and antibody abnormalities. There seems to be reasonable evidence that three different researches have isolated an abnormal alpha-2-globulin from the blood of schizophrenic individuals. This abnormal protein impairs the ability of rats to perform a previously learned task. It is indicative of the problems of biochemical research in schizophrenia that after the abnormal protein was isolated, its level was then discovered to be no higher in schizophrenic patients than in control subjects. Luckily, in this case we possessed the more sophisticated techniques alluded to earlier, and when the physical structure of the protein was investigated it was discovered that the shape of the molecule from a schizophrenic plasma was indeed very different from the shape in normal controls. As fascinating and as definite as this abnormal protein seems to be, its actual importance is as yet unestablished. As one of its principal investigators has stated, there is as yet no proof that the abnormal protein, or any of its biochemical effects, are directly implicated in the etiology of schizophrenia.

The status of our present knowledge has not provided us with answers. We are in a peculiar position of knowing that something is there to be discovered, but not being able to specifically define what it is. The currently held and apparently validated notions about transmethylation and abnormal proteins may be vulnerable to the fate of many previous findings and may be discarded in a few years. Even assuming that the specific deficit or deficits can be found, we may still not have a cure for schizophrenia. All of our knowledge about the biochemistry of diabetes has not helped us to cure the disease but only to manage it more successfully.

Chapter 10

❧❧❧❧❧❧❧❧

Experiential Theories

Since dynamic psychiatry began with the discoveries of Charcot and Freud, descriptions of psychological mechanisms for coping and adjusting have been elaborated and a number of theories have been developed that attempt to explain the cause of schizophrenia in terms of life experiences. These theories of etiology of schizophrenia are related to the many theories of child growth and development and systems of human motivation.

The first group of such theories relates the cause of schizophrenia to a specific event. Such proposed events include abandonment or rejection by the significant mothering figure in the earliest months of life. Support for such a theory has been obtained from the histories of adult schizophrenic patients as well as from the work of René Spitz, who first studied marasmus in infants residing in the nursery for newborns (see Spitz and Cobliner, 1966). His study demonstrated that newborn infants who are cared for in the sterile although otherwise excellent nursery of a foundling home do not survive as well as infants reared by their own mothers, even though their mothers were not particularly suitable for the task of child rearing and the infants were cared for in poor conditions in a jail. The infants in the foundling home had a high death rate and showed some symptoms that had vague similarity to later schizophrenic conditions. Related to both the adult historical material and the observation of the effects of abandonment in newborn infants is the unique experimental work that has been used to explain early rejection as the central experiential cause for schizophrenia. Animals who were deprived of natural affectionate mothering in early life tended to develop problems similar to those of human schizophrenia. Harlow's monkeys demonstrated permanent personality change when reared on surrogate wire mothers (Harlow, 1959). The monkeys showed severe disorganization in anxiety management and intermonkey relationships. The problem with all the theories that attempt to relate the cause of schizophrenia to a specific event occurring early in life is the tendency of history to be distorted. We must remember that history is constantly being rewritten. When you ask me about my childhood, if I am feeling bad about myself and if my self-esteem is terribly impaired, and if I cannot remember ever feeling better, then I will tell you about all the rejections and deprivations I have had or thought I have had. These rejections are real, these are what I will focus on when I am sick. On the other hand, when I am feeling well I will tell you about the good things that happened to me. Anecdotal material from earliest childhood is a totally unreliable way of obtaining information about child-rearing experiences during the early years. Direct observation of children is also difficult. We have no way of knowing what the child is thinking until the child can verbalize. We also do not know what animals think. Animal experimental results that are used to explain the etiology of human schizophrenia require anthropomorphizing.

A second group of theories is based on significant conditions in the life of the future schizophrenic patient. One of the most colorful theories of this group is that of the "schizophrenogenic mother." In this view, schizophrenia in adults is caused by being reared by a schizophrenogenic mother who gives confusing signals, who does not fondle and cuddle properly, who cannot transmit security, comfort, and continuity. The schizophrenogenic mother is someone who cannot give supportive care competently in the first few years of life.

Melanie Klein (1961), in a similar theory, has related the onset of schizophrenia to the feeding interaction between mother and child. She describes the stony breast from which the child attempts to get nourishment but from which the child can only develop a paranoid position. Overwhelming difficulties even in adult life have been thought to cause schizophrenia.

Among the experiential theories of etiology there are a number that relate the cause of schizophrenia to specific interactions. The best known of these is the Bateson double-bind theory. Bateson (1960) proposed that the individual who is caught in a field of double-binding from which he cannot escape, particularly in childhood, learns to react to such an intolerable situation by learning how to be schizophrenic, or, as others have said, by learning to schizophrene. There are many similar theories proposing that the individual learns to "go crazy" during intolerable situations in the maturational years as an alternative way of coping. The double bind is only one such situation. Other situations include early overwhelming responsibility, sexual betrayal by a significant adult, and disorganization and chaos caused in family disintegration.

Identification with an individual who is schizophrenic is another proposed "cause" of schizophrenia. A daughter of a schizophrenic mother (who is different from the schizophrenogenic mother) might internalize the parent with the schizophrenic condition. It has been said that a schizophrenogenic family is one where the identification and the object ingestion become so split and so disorganized as to give rise to schizophrenic illness.

Many theorists propose that schizophrenia is a maturational error. Freud's original idea, that schizophrenia was a narcissistic neurosis in which the individual never developed beyond primary narcissism, is a theory of maturational error. If the human personality as it is formed misses specific maturational steps, the individual cannot develop the necessary ego structure, self-boundaries, self-esteem, or trusting relationship in himself or in significant others.

Schizophrenia can also be viewed as the result of a perceptual disorder, in which errors in perception are caused by life experience or by biochemical errors. The resulting disorganization of perception becomes the basis of the schizophrenic illness. Secondary to his perceptual disorder, the schizophrenic patient has problems in thinking and in feeling, and has defects in the management of anxiety and in relating to others. German phenomenologists and French categorical phenomenologists have approached the understanding of psychopathology from that point of view. The perception of time, space, and causality has been found to be altered in schizophrenic patients. Such theorists explain all of the other signs and symptoms of schizophrenia as secondary to perceptual alteration.

There is a group of theorists who view schizophrenia as an experience but not as an illness. Perhaps the most popular view is the theory suggested by Laing (1965). He proposes that schizophrenia is a special form of growing, developing, and relating. He feels that this maturational process, which has painful signs and symptoms, is a way for the individual to grow, to develop, to learn about himself, and to mature. Other theorists do see schizophrenia as an illness but also think of it as a growth state much like adolescence. It is thus a state in which there is a differential dystonic growth, in which ego boundaries have not been adequately developed, and in which the pain and agony of the growing pains is severe. Such theorists have quipped that adolescence is the sickness from which most of us recover; those of us who do not, we call *schizophrenic*. There is some truth in the observation that the normal stress, confusion, and lability of adolescence have some similarity to schizophrenia. Even some of the projective test results in stressed adolescents are similar to those seen in schizophrenic patients. In a specific psychotic episode in an adolescent person, it may be difficult to tell whether we are dealing with a situational reaction or the first onset of a schizophrenic illness, but the experienced clinician using an historical approach to diagnosis can tell the difference between the schizophrenic person and the adolescent.

Among the psychological theories of schizophrenia is the existential approach. Ludwig Binswanger, Medard Boss, and our group (American Existential Psychiatry) look at the world and life space of the schizophrenic person as we look at the world of all human beings. Each of us creates his own world by projecting himself and his internal structure. After we create our world, we live in it. If we have certain basic defects of existence, we create a world that has the same defects; then we live painfully and unsuccessfully in that world. The major defect in the schizophrenic world is the distressing emptiness. Schizophrenic persons have described themselves as empty holes, as bathtubs without a plug that require constant filling—as soon as the filling stops they are empty again. Such patients see themselves as having an internal vacuum that is painful and that threatens to implode at any moment, collapsing their whole self-structure in a heap of rubble. Schizophrenic existence is agonizing, empty, and is a gnawing nothingness. The world is created as empty, echoing and hollow, peopled rather than populated. Ghosts from the past and specters of the future dance in the present—in a moment of action in which there is no flow of time from past or from future into the present. Such a world is the stage of the agony and distress of the schizophrenic human being. The attempts at restitution by such patients are attempts to fill the hole, stuff the emptiness, prevent the implosion of the vacuum. The pain and agony, the dread and fear, the failing anxiety management and the interpersonal misadventures are all aspects of the empty individual living his existence as a hole in an empty world of vacuum and nothingness.

All of the experiential theories of schizophrenia can be presented as attractive proposals for explaining experiences leading to the onset of this lifelong illness. However, when we attempt rigorous anecdotal investigation it becomes clear that not all patients who are diagnosed as schizophrenic have such experiences. When we attempt to create an experimental design in which the experiences producing schizophrenia can be tested by attempting to predict schizophrenia in adults where certain experiences have occurred in childhood, the results do not support the theories. One always has to postulate an X factor, one always has to come back to the understanding that schizophrenia is the final outcome of a multitude of factors: experience, genetics, learned behavior, biochemistry, and much more. We have to ask a new question and we have to develop a new approach to thinking about this illness if we are to pursue effective and logical research and treatment.

Chapter 11

⅋⅋⅋⅋⅋⅋⅋⅋

A Proposal for the 1970s

In the second half of the 1970s, psychiatry faces the problem of schizophrenia without the discovery of a specific etiology and without a generally accepted definition. The medical model of schizophrenia has been severely criticized by some who have focused on the social, political, and therapeutic misuses of labels and on the mistreatment of some schizophrenic patients.

Of the models available to explain and to understand the disabilities called *schizophrenia,* the medical model works as well as any other and somewhat better than most. Its logical response to the problem of schizophrenia is treatment, including education, social remedy, prevention, and persuasion.

In spite of the problem of having many unknowns in our understanding of schizophrenia, we do have an identifiable set of disabilities. Approximately 1 percent of the world population with these disabilities face the problems of living in an identifiable and predictable way. Life with these disabilities can be understood and has a describable natural history. Problems in the lives of schizophrenic people can be understood as secondary to these disabilities.

In 1976, we can say that there is an identifiable set of disabilities leading to a describable sequence of life problems following a predictable natural history that we call *schizophrenia*. This identifiable set of disabilities leading to problems in living, following a predictable course, can be described and understood as an illness. It fits the characteristics of an illness and even though the "lesion" has not been found, there is no model that fits the observable events more clearly than the medical model. Even beyond such a logical approach, from a pragmatic point of view, the medical model allows for more enlightened and benign interventions than any other model.

As the medical profession has been concerned with the relief of pain and dysfunction, this concern is suitable for the treatment of schizophrenia. The educational model is concerned with implanting knowledge; the social model, with abolishing inequities and changing social conditions; the religious model, with a system of ethics; and the legal model, with the definition and abolishment of crime. None of these models and their interventions is as benign and practical as the medical model.

We come to the conclusion that in 1976 the most logical approach and the most suitable model, leading to the most helpful kind of intervention, is the medical model. Yet we must also look at some of the problems within the medical model. Thomas Szasz, an outspoken critic, has made us aware of some of the misapplications and social injustices that can be created within the medical model. He points out (1963) some of the logical errors caused by confusing brain disease with mental illness. He alerts us to the semantic problems of talking about disorganized behavior and behavioral dysfunction as though they were illnesses. However, the problems go beyond such issues of logic.

The common use of the medical model, particularly as applied to physical (anatomical and physiological) disease, results in not holding the sick individual responsible for his volitional acts. Our legal system reflects this attitude. If someone engages in antisocial behavior and it can be proven that he is mentally ill, he is judged not guilty. Similarly, if any one of us engages in behavior for which we wish to avoid responsibility, one of the easiest ways to do so is to say, "I was not myself"; "I don't know what got into me"; "It is my upbringing"; or "It is my neurosis or my psychosis, not me." Yet such clear misuses of the medical model by individuals is an argument not against the medical model, but against its misuse. This misuse is not dissimilar to many other problems of human society. It is not guns or cars that kill people; it is people who use guns and cars carelessly. It makes as little sense for someone to say, "I didn't mean to hit you, it was my psychosis that did it," as it would be to say, "I didn't mean to run through the red light and kill you, it was my car that did it." The problems of society created by the use of the medical model in understanding human behavior in function and dysfunction, in health and in illness, are just that: the problems of society, not of the medical model. The same kinds of problems would occur in the educational model, in the social model, or in the religious model.

Changes reflecting our altered understanding of schizophrenia have occurred in the medical model over the past hundred years. At the end of the nineteenth century, the basic model of scientific medicine was proposed by Robert Koch, a German bacteriologist who had discovered the etiology of tuberculosis in his description and discovery of the acid-fast bacillus. He proposed four postulates stating that we know the etiology of the disease if we can fulfill certain criteria: (1) we must first describe the disease in detail and isolate the disease-causing organism from the diseased host and grow it in pure culture; (2) we must then take the identified and isolated pathogenic organism and inject it into a healthy host; (3) the disease process must be reproduced in the previously healthy host; and (4) the pathogenic organism must again be isolated and identified and must be the same as the organism injected into the healthy host. Koch proposed that if we fulfilled these four postulates we can then know the cause of an illness.

Since Koch's time we have discovered that the problem of

disease etiology is much more complex. It is far too simple a solution to say that tuberculosis is caused by the tubercle bacillus. Tuberculosis is a complex disease. Resistance, genetic predisposition, emotional state, nutritional state, social situations, family living conditions, hypersensitivity to the bacteria, and personality type, in conjunction with the presence of the tubercle bacillus, lead to the clinical picture of tuberculosis. If all of the conditions come together and create a picture that looks like clinical tuberculosis, but the tubercle bacillus cannot be found, then we call the condition a different disease. The Koch model of disease included only one of the relevant etiological factors and did not take into account all of the conditions coming together.

In early dynamic psychiatry, Freud and his colleagues used the Koch model in looking for a specific causative agent of mental illness. It could be the presence of the spirochete in the brain (in central nervous system syphilis) or a specific trauma occurring in childhood (as was postulated by Charcot and in the early work of Freud). The same kind of problems occurred in psychiatric illness as in understanding tuberculosis. The question was "If rejection by the mother during the first six months of life causes schizophrenia, why does schizophrenia occur only in a small number of people who have had that specific trauma?" In answering such questions one always ends up by postulating an X factor or a multitude of factors that, taken together with the specific trauma, lead to the picture of the illness. These factors can only be described retrospectively.

After the Koch model came the model of diseases of adaptation, primarily stimulated by the work of Hans Selye (1952). In physiological and anatomical disease it was discovered that the adaptation model of the disease would add much to the understanding of certain illnesses, perhaps all illnesses. The disease process itself and much of the dysfunction and discomfort caused by the disease were attempts at coping with or defending against stress. The failing attempt at adaptation becomes the disease process itself. People do become ill not because of the bacteremia but because of the response to the bacteremia consisting of the pain, the swelling, the redness, and the rise in temperature (*dolor, tumor, rubor,* and *calor*). These factors become the signs and symptoms of the disease.

Similarly, in psychiatry the failing defense mechanisms were understood as the illness, the maladaptive response of normal adaptive mechanisms. Neurosis was understood as the excessive or maladaptive attempt at dealing with anxiety by use of normal defense mechanisms, normal adaptive mechanisms, and normal anxiety management mechanisms. In our understanding of psychosis, we began to see that many of the signs and symptoms resulted from failing psychological mechanisms for maintaining homeostasis, for coping with psychological pain, or for dealing with discomfort. Symptoms were seen as restitutive and the illness itself was a giant attempt at restitution. That model of adaptation became the major model in psychiatry, and schizophrenia was seen as a reaction to stress.

Today, both in medicine and psychiatry, we are aware of the limitations of both of these models of disease. We have found that we must change the questions we ask. The new model of disease and the new question are based on the work of Harold Wolff and Stewart Wolf (1942), which was begun in their pivotal studies of the etiology of peptic ulcer. Their model was called the "theory of the relevant etiological factor." They proposed that we can no longer ask the question "What causes this illness?" Rather, we must substitute a different question. The new question is "What conditions taken *together* in *this individual* at *this time* make it possible for these symptoms to emerge?" This formulation implies that other conditions coming together in the individual would not result in the same clinical picture. Also, the same conditions coming together at another time in the individual may not result in the same clinical picture, and the same conditions in another individual may not result in the same clinical picture.

This different and new question opens many doors to research and allows us to develop a sensible treatment approach even when we do not know the "cause" of schizophrenia. We attempt to identify conditions in the biological areas, the genetic aspects, the family relationships, the economic factors, the psychological functions, and the social interactions. We then ask "What conditions taken together, what family structure, what psychological state, what biological factors, what genetic predisposition, what social conditions, what religious upbringing, and what economic problems, all taken together in this individual at this time have come together to create this clinical picture?" The second part of the question then becomes "Which of these situations can we alter to change the clinical picture and to develop a treatment intervention?"

The result of this new question is that we view schizophrenia as a very complex psychobiological disease that we can observe, that we can describe. Many of the factors observed and described can be altered. We can intervene psychologically, with psychotherapy and retraining. We can intervene biologically, with medication, diet, and exercise. We can intervene socially, through environmental changes. We can intervene in the family, with family therapy. We can intervene economically, with vocational rehabilitation and training. Soon we will even be able to intervene genetically.

Today, in 1976, we see schizophrenia as a psychobiological disease that has a clearly identifiable set of disabilities, that has a describable sequence of problems and a predictable natural history throughout the life of the patient. Our description of schizophrenia illness is aided by using the medical model based on the theory of the relevant etiological factor. Instead of asking what causes this illness we now must ask what conditions, taken together in this individual at this time, make it possible for this clinical picture to emerge. Using this medical model allows us to develop a rational treatment approach, multifaceted in its interventions, employing all of the many skills we have in helping professions in maximizing comfort and function and in minimizing distress and dysfunction.

Chapter 12

≋≋≋≋≋≋≋≋

Theory of Treatment

The treatment of the schizophrenic patient must take into account the major difficulties inflicted on the person by this disease. Treatment consists of rescue during the crisis phase and rehabilitation in the long-term supportive care. We must suppress the pain, discomfort, and dysfunction and must provide rehabilitation in its widest sense to help the individual to live his life with more ease, comfort, effectiveness, and pleasure.

Because the patient cannot manage anxiety, the resulting unboundedness of that anxiety causes serious consequences that become symptoms. The exhaustion from his clumsy and ineffective attempt to deal with it causes him further symptoms as part of his restitutive effort. The problem of treating this failure of anxiety management must be approached from three vantage points: (1) we lessen the experience of anxiety by chemical intervention; (2) we rearrange the life space of the individual and his psychosocial environment in such a way as to decrease and avoid the situations that for him produce anxiety; and (3) we teach him new, more effective, and less expensive ways of managing his anxiety.

A great deal has been written about the use of medication in the treatment of schizophrenia. Our younger colleagues tend to forget that even before the availability of modern tranquilizers there were useful medications to help individuals with their discomfort and dysfunction in psychosis. The older medications, which included sedatives, bromides, opiates, narcotics, and hypnotics, all were effective in lessening the experience of anxiety and gave the patient an adaptive rest from coping with its inherent problems. This allowed for some personality reorganization when there was less bombardment of the coping faculties (ego) by anxiety. The side effects of these medications, however, were major. They put the patient to sleep and made him nonfunctional so that the pharmacotherapy was not practical for chronic illnesses such as schizophrenia. At the turn of the century, the Germans succeeded in using a kind of sleep therapy that seemed to offer some considerable benefit for acute psychotic episodes. This treatment consisted of giving the adaptive capacities of the personality a rest by putting the patient to sleep for two weeks. Many patients at the end of the two weeks seemed to have benefited from such therapy, seemed to be able to reorganize, and seemed to have made a good recovery from the acute episode. However, when we are dealing with a chronic illness such as schizophrenia, the sleep therapy becomes much less effective except as a technique of rescue from the acute episodes. Even today there is reason on occasion to attempt a variant of sleep therapy during acute episodes, and there is some evidence that this treatment can offer considerable benefit in the rescue from crisis.

In the 1950s, with the discovery of chlorpromazine as the first important tranquilizer, the treatment of schizophrenia became a major concern for psychopharmacology. Since that discovery, and since the even earlier use of reserpine (rauwolfia alkaloid) during the prior decade, there has been a constant stream of new compounds developed for the treatment of schizophrenia. Now there are literally dozens of tranquilizers and tranquilizer combinations, each of which has been found to be of some value in the treatment of schizophrenia.

But we know that many of the claims made for the tranquilizers are incorrect. Some of them were clearly the result of a need for advertising a new product. For example, Thorazine is a good tranquilizer that, if given in adequate dosages for a particular individual, will lower the level of anxiety. As the anxiety level is lowered, there is some reorganization of thought processes and some considerable diminution of all of the restitutional symptoms and those symptoms that are sequential to anxiety. Because this reduction of sequential and restitutional symptoms occurs, it has been erroneously assumed that the tranquilizers are specific for the treatment of schizophrenia.

One of the next major tranquilizers that was advertised into popular use was Stelazine (trifluoperazine). Since Thorazine had been so successful with the hyperactive agitated patients and since no drug had been specifically designed for the withdrawn and slowed patient, Stelazine was pushed as the drug of choice. It was even used as an "antidepressant," which it certainly is not.

Another drug coming onto the scene was Compazine (prochlorperazine). As no medication had been advertised for the non-psychotic anxious patient, soon Compazine was developed as the drug of choice for the neurotic anxious patient. Since then, there have been hundreds of claims for specific drugs having specific effects. None of these claims is borne out when carefully evaluated.

At the time of this writing, we can designate all of the tranquilizers of value in the treatment of schizophrenia as being effective in the treatment of the anxiety that occurs in schizophrenia. These tranquilizers are all about equally effective. The choice of drug really depends on the choice of side effects. Some tend to produce many extrapyramidal side effects or to have sedative action. Others produce anticholinergic complications. The therapist chooses that medication that causes the least bothersome side effects for the particular individual to be treated.

There is no evidence whatsoever that mixtures of phenothiazines are any better than single-drug administration. There is some very recent evidence that after many years of being on a phenothiazine some chronic schizophrenic patients seem to get along better without medication. However, this work is still in its early stages and the data are not yet available to tell us whether this phenomenon is related to the length of time of taking phenothiazines, the length of illness, or the age of the patient.

In general, it is an accepted therapeutic technique to keep schizophrenic patients for the rest of their lives on the drug that has helped to rescue them from crisis and that has maintained them over long-term supportive care. Some authorities advocate an occasional drug vacation, perhaps one month per year, if this vacation can be effected without leading to a major disorganization for the patient. There is also some evidence that such an occasional drug vacation can prevent some of the long-term complications of chronic phenothiazine medication (such as tardive dyskinesia). Patients who have schizophrenia, which is a chronic disease by definition, generally do better if they take adequate amounts of phenothiazine over long periods.

In choosing the specific drug to be used, it is very important for us to recognize that individuals respond differently to the drugs. These responses are not entirely predictable from statistical studies. We should be prepared to switch medication if a particular patient is not responding and if we have gone through the proper steps of evaluating his response (see Chapter 13).

The second part of the treatment approach to the disability of anxiety management is to make changes in the environment and psychosocial space of the individual patient so that he can avoid situations that for him trigger anxiety. This change can only be made by getting to know the patient thoroughly, by having explored with the patient in detail the course of his illness, and by having identified with the patient all those situations in which his anxiety is triggered. By taking a very careful history and exploring with both the patient and the significant others in his life, the therapist can begin to identify the patient's anxiety-producing situations. Although we must remind ourselves that patients differ, some of these situations can be generalized for most patients suffering from schizophrenia. Interpersonal transactions are the most taxing and most difficult for schizophrenic patients, particularly those relationships that demand closeness. Even though this observation is borne out by clinical facts, we must constantly remember that although one schizophrenic person has some similarity to another schizophrenic person, he is also quite different. We cannot assume that it is always the interpersonal transaction or the demands for closeness or intimacy that should be avoided.

The detailed history provides both the patient and the therapist with a picture of the kinds of situations, the types of relationships, the activities and the feeling states that lead to major heightening of anxiety for the individual. Once these areas have been identified, carefully mapped out, and thoroughly understood, they can be used to guide the patient away from circumstances that are beyond his emotional means. Patients can learn to accept limitations. One of the important aspects of living in comfort and with considerable function and some pleasure in spite of schizophrenia is to learn to accept these limitations. An important part of the chronic supportive care is to teach the patient these specific limitations for him and to get him to accept these limitations and to live his life accordingly. Just as the diabetic must learn that although others can eat sugar without difficulty he must avoid it, so the schizophrenic can learn that certain kinds of identifiable circumstances are beyond his emotional means because of his illness. If he can learn to identify these, to structure his life to avoid them, then he will have less difficulty in living. Whatever feelings he develops about having to accept these limitations must also be handled in therapy. This approach does not mean the schizophrenic person lives like a cripple or an invalid but that he identifies his specific limitations, knowing that every one of us also has certain limitations.

There are other important facts about anxiety that can be learned and that the patient can use as techniques of coping. If the patient has reviewed in some considerable detail the past history of his periods of disorganization, he can usually see a series of early warning signs when they are about to occur. If the patient can learn to identify his specific signs of disorganization, then he has a second line of defense. First we should teach him to avoid those situations that are beyond his emotional means and that lead to increasing anxiety and subsequently to psychotic disorganization. If he misses these or if new ones crop up, then he can use the learned signs of disorganization. He can train himself in emergency procedures to back off from situations at that point so as to avoid further disorganization into psychosis.

The third aspect in the rehabilitation of the disability of anxiety management also requires detailed historical material. We identify the habitual anxiety management techniques (defense mechanisms, coping mechanisms) used by the patient and the sequence in which they are used. We identify those that seem to work better than others. We identify those that lead to symptoms rather than to anxiety binding as well as those that seem excessively expensive to the total person. On the basis of such an historical review, we then develop a plan for techniques of anxiety management that particularly fit an individual patient. We train the patient in the use of these techniques. This training is done in the therapeutic transaction, within the matrix of the interpersonal therapeutic situation or within the milieu of the controlled treatment situation such as in the day-care center, in the crisis team, in group therapy, or in the hospital milieu. Such training in anxiety management, which is always part of psychotherapeutic interventions, is most useful when it is geared to the specific patient's needs and when it is practiced and reinforced by giving the patient experience. The schizophrenic patient does not need the insight from his psychotherapy; he needs experience. He does not need the understanding, he needs the activity.

The second nuclear disability in schizophrenia, the interpersonal failure, requires a treatment approach specifically based on the therapeutic relationship. In schizophrenic existences, interpersonal relationships are characterized by clumsiness, ineffectiveness, and disastrous outcome. These interpersonal problems are part of the basic disability of any schizophrenic existence. The approach to rehabilitating for this disability is to teach the patient to avoid certain interpersonal transactions that he cannot possibly manage. We also help him to learn techniques with which he can manage interpersonal transactions more effectively and with which he can appear "as if" he were able to relate nonschizophrenically to other people. We attempt to arrange interpersonal treatment transactions having a chance of success in spite of the patient's clumsiness and difficulty. The patient is offered the treatment experience to build his self-esteem and to learn new techniques of interacting that can be generalized to life. This stage is a most difficult part of the treatment because the very problems that are the schizophrenic illness also become the difficulty in treatment.

The therapeutic relationship, whether it is with an individual, a group or an organization (clinic, hospital, profession), must be arranged to serve as the matrix of the treatment transaction. It is through the therapeutic relationship that medication is administered, that training of the patient for anxiety management and interpersonal relationships is carried out. It is through the supportive relationship that the patient gets comfort and learns to elaborate his life.

The therapeutic relationship must first of all be characterized by being nonjudgmental and nondemanding. This requirement does not mean that in the relationship the therapist does not make judgments as to what is acceptable and what is not acceptable behavior, nor does it mean that he is not willing to say what is real and what is unreal. It does mean that the consequences of past and contemplated future actions are explored with the patient to help him to recognize whether the outcome will be desirable or undesirable for him. The relationship is nondemanding in terms of not requiring the patient to be successful. It is demanding in terms of requiring the patient to keep his appointments and to be with the therapist at specified times. The demands for success in functions that are made by middle-class society, by family, and by the patient's own needs must in fact be softened for the patient if he cannot meet them.

Aside from being nondemanding and nonjudgmental, the therapeutic relationship must be characterized by an ongoingness that keeps the future open and that does not lead to or threaten termination. The relationship must not promise more than it can deliver and it must not threaten to terminate when the patient is "well." The relationship must be reliable and always available. The therapist must demonstrate this availability and reliability over and over again. He must make himself available to the patient for the process of identification. This approach requires that the patient take measure of his therapist, know something about him as a person, and be able to ingest him (in psychoanalytic terms), to use him as an archaic, primitive, internalized object. The therapist must take many steps and use techniques to be available for the patient (to remain within the patient) and to nurture the therapeutic alliance. The specific techniques required to allow for the patient's use of the therapist as an identity model become part of providing long-term support.

The interpersonal relationship within the therapeutic transaction is used to connect the patient with his past and his future, which then results in the establishment of some faith in the flow of time. If this connection with the past and future is established, the patient can function more comfortably and more effectively. He can increase his self-esteem and decrease the amount of energy it takes to go through the day. Rehabilitation to correct for the interpersonal disabilities of schizophrenia will also correct the disability of historicity, which becomes such an important and devastating problem in the life of the schizophrenic person.

One aspect of the failure of the interpersonal relationships is that again the schizophrenic person tends to get into situations that are beyond his emotional means. It is one of the important functions of the therapist to get the patient off the hook, to get him out of impossible situations whenever necessary. This function, too, is one of the cornerstones of the long-term treatment of schizophrenia. The patient does not need failures in his interpersonal transactions. He needs successes. One of the ways to avoid further failures is to prevent him from committing himself to relationships that are obviously beyond his emotional means. Whenever a patient tells us that he is going to take a new job, get involved in a new and more complex relationship, or change his life situation, we must respond by helping the patient *not to have to do it*. After careful exploration of all aspects of the reality of the situation and the possible consequences of the contemplated action, we must allow the patient to back out gracefully while at the same time giving him permission to go ahead. But it must always be understood that no matter how this particular venture comes out, the therapist will be available and will be a source of support for the patient. In this way the therapist gives permission to the patient to be different and not to attempt to be like everyone else. The therapist helps him to accept his alienation and difference and to live within certain limitations.

It is also within the matrix of the therapeutic transaction that we help the patient with problems in reality testing. The selective attention and inattention to what the patient tells will help him to differentiate clearly between reality and action, on the one hand, and fantasy, delusions, hallucinations, and unreality on the other. By focusing on consensually validated reality rather than allowing the patient to focus on his own autistic reality we help him to make that differentiation. This approach does not mean that we depreciate the patient's own personal reality. We merely let him know that he must learn to differentiate it from consensually validated reality. The arranged experience of therapeutic trans-actions, both in groups and individually, in the hospital milieu and day care, teaches the patient that a relationship can be counted on, that the world can be seen as a somewhat reliable place, and that interpersonal space can be maintained in a comfortable way without too much closeness or too much distance. In this way the interper-sonal relationship of the therapeutic transaction can become a train-ing ground for teaching interpersonal styles with which the patient can be comfortable. All of this presupposes that our treatment techniques also address themselves to the disability of the failing historicity.

The failure of historicity makes every situation new. Every day is lived as the first day of the patient's life, every relationship is the first one of its kind. Yet certain experiences can be arranged in treatment that counteract this failure of historicity. All of these experiences occur in the matrix of the interpersonal transaction. However, this interpersonal therapeutic transaction must be very special, must use many very concrete signposts of ongoingness, and must supply constant reiteration, reinforcement, and nourishment of the relationship. All of these treatment techniques are designed to reestablish the flow of time. For example, for many patients the ongoingness of the relationship, not as an abstraction but as a concrete series of events, helps to counteract the failure of his-toricity. The patient comes for his therapy appointment. If he does not appear, the therapist goes out and gets him. If necessary, the therapist calls him and reminds him or sends him a letter or postcard to remind him where to be and when to be there. During the therapy appointment, the patient is concretely reminded of the prior appointment and he is told some of the things that were discussed and planned at that time. He is asked to tell what has happened since the last appointment and how the plans that were formulated have worked out. Then he is told of the next appointment. Plans are made about activities during the interim. These plans may be done in writing, with both the patient and the therapist having a list of what needs to be done. Most important, at the termination of the appointment the patient gets a slip that shows the therapist's name, and the time and place of the next appointment. In this way the therapeutic contact is extended into the past and into the future, using very concrete techniques in an attempt to reestablish the flow of time. In between appointments the therapist may have telephone or letter contact, or brief personal contact, to keep the relationship going. This approach tends to keep the experience of the therapeutic relationship "sticking to the ribs" of the patient.

There are other techniques used to accomplish this continuity. The patient may carry a picture of the hospital or of the therapist or of the clinic. He may carry a talisman such as a bottle of pills with a label containing his name, his file number, the therapist's name, to remind him of the relationship when he has "forgotten" it exists, to reinforce the relationship and the flow of time. All of these techniques are used to counteract the failure of historicity.

For many patients who are terribly uncomfortable in the interpersonal transaction and who find it difficult to sit and talk in an office, activity is a more concrete vehicle for a relationship. With many such patients we have found it useful to take walks, eat lunch, engage in physical activity (playing ping-pong, going for a ride, doing errands, helping him to enroll in a class and going to his first class with him, going to his wedding, and so on). Since such joint activities by the patient and the therapist reinforce the relationship and maintain the availability of that relationship, these activities are particularly suitable for the treatment of schizophrenia. All of these techniques that counteract the failure of historicity are based on keeping the therapeutic relationship going, on allowing the patient to use the therapeutic relationship, even when the therapist is not there in person, for as long as possible. Once the patient is through the crisis, once the major task of supportive care is done, the teaching and training of anxiety management and supportive care to supply the necessary reinforcement can be handled by a very occasional appointment. Often a patient needs to have appointments only once a month, and there are patients for whom once a year is enough.

The therapist can use the interpersonal therapeutic transaction to rehabilitate the patient in such a way that the patient can compensate for his failure in historicity by connecting the patient with his past and his future. This approach establishes the flow of time. The techniques of treatment that deal with the problem of historicity include the planning of activities for the patient, giving appointment slips, reviewing the events of the prior week, and engaging in joint activities to express the ongoingness and constancy of the therapeutic relationship.

The strategy of treatment of schizophrenia is based on the disease model of the relevant etiological factor. After we ask the question "What identifiable factors in this individual's life at this time cause his pain, his agony, his difficulty and disability?" we can begin to design the treatment. First we list these factors for the individual. We list the psychological failures and dysfunctions, the difficulties and strengths. We list the economic situation of his life as it relates both to his problems and to his abilities. We list the familial factors, the social factors, the interpersonal factors, the genetic factors. We list the vocational factors, the educational factors, the racial and cultural factors, the social class determinants. In each of these areas we list the disabilities as well as the abilities and strengths. When designing a treatment program for any patient, it is more important to catalog his abilities and his assets than his disabilities, dysfunction, and pain. In making his life better, we need to work with that portion of him that represents his strengths. We need to suppress his disadvantages and discomforts.

From such a multifaceted treatment approach, we will discover in each schizophrenic life many factors that can be altered by intervention. Biologically we intervene with medication. Economically we intervene by changing the financial situation. Psychologically we intervene by teaching anxiety-managing devices, by offering a supporting relationship, and by helping the patient to learn techniques of identifying disorganization when it occurs. Socially and in the family we intervene by environmental manipulation. Donald Langsley has shown how family crisis treatment during acute psychosis is a technique that results in better outcome than traditional hospital treatment. Often, giving support to the family of a schizophrenic person will cause a major shift in the psychosocial space of that person; he will improve and be able to function so much better that the family thinks he is "cured." Yet the only change has been the family's changing so that the patient can take on a different role in the family structure. Intervening vocationally by helping the patient to be trained for and get employment can make a major difference in the life of the schizophrenic person. In all of these multifaceted approaches to the treatment of an individual schizophrenic life, the purpose is to increase function, comfort, and pleasure. Again, when such a program is well-designed and effectively carried out, the patient can improve so much that the remission from the acute symptoms gives him the appearance of having been "cured." His disabilities can be so well compensated for that it appears "as if" he can manage his anxiety effectively and inexpensively, "as if" he can relate nonschizophrenically, and "as if" he has intact historicity. Such a state has led to the concept of the "as if" person, developed by Helene Deutsch, (1942), which refers to the successful rehabilitation of the person so that it appears "as if" he were not schizophrenic.

Chapter 13

≈≈≈≈≈≈≈≈

Treating the Patient in Crisis

Crisis treatment must be timely and effective. This requirement is of the utmost importance for four reasons.

First, it is usually during the crisis that the patient comes to the attention of the helping profession for intervention and rescue. It is during crisis treatment that the therapeutic alliance is established, which forms the lifelong relationship with the helping situation. During crisis intervention we can teach the individual how to use helping resources. For this reason alone it is crucial that crisis intervention be well thought out, be effective, and be sensibly designed for taking on an individual who is chronically ill and who will have future crises and future remissions.

The second reason why crisis intervention must be timely and effective is that we must rescue the patient from pain and agony, from dysfunction and difficulty, as quickly as possible. We need to effect this rescue rapidly not only for humanitarian reasons but also to prevent difficulties with which the patient or the family might have to live. The most obvious of these difficulties would be successful suicide. Other serious consequences are the kinds of behavior that result in hostile attitudes of others toward the patient, in turn making it difficult for him to live in his psychosocial space. If we do not prevent the person in crisis from acting in a way that is interpreted by others as dangerous or totally crazy, or as self-destructive, he has to live with these attitudes and consequences from then on. How previous crises have been handled determines the intervention in future crises. The most important factor in prescribing hospitalization is prior hospitalization. The most important factor in deciding that the patient is potentially dangerous is his having been called *dangerous* previously. It is important for us to save the patient from himself and for himself, from engaging in behavior that will alienate others from him and that will create a history with which it is difficult for him to live.

The third observation of major importance in crisis intervention is that during the crisis we teach the patient how to be "crazy." If we allow him to retreat into the hospital during the crisis, if we allow him to handle periods of stress and anxiety and disorganization and dysfunction by retreating into a long period of helplessness and hopelessness, we are in fact creating a situation of chronicity of symptoms (to be distinguished from chronicity of illness) that will determine future handling of stress and the course of the patient's illness and symptoms. In many of our helping institutions in the mental health network, we teach the patient ways of being crazy. Many of the procedures used in emergency rooms of psychiatric hospitals tend to reinforce craziness rather than noncrazy behavior. When the patient is upset, acting crazy, he gets a lot of both negative and positive attention. As he calms down and acts less crazy, attention is withdrawn and he has to give up being the focus of the ward or the emergency room to someone else who comes in screaming louder or being more disorganized. What better way could there be of letting the frightened, disorganized patient in crisis know that acting crazy gets attention while pulling together and acting less crazy results in the withdrawal of attention?

A fourth reason for paying meticulous attention to providing effective and logical crisis intervention is to relieve pain and suffering. As we have said repeatedly throughout this book, schizophrenia is a chronic and lifelong illness. Once it has appeared and been diagnosed, we may anticipate that the basic disabilities and difficulties will continue for the life of the patient. Our job is to minimize the pain and suffering during crises, to establish the proper long-term supporting relationship for the helping situation that will prevent and abort as many future crises as possible, and to teach the patient techniques of handling his life in such a way that he does not have to have crises. All these interventions are begun during the first crisis intervention, when the person first comes to the attention of the helping situation.

Rescue is the focus of crisis intervention. The patient comes to us in crisis, pain, and disorganization, showing major manifestations of his three disabilities and many of the sequential and restitutional symptoms of these disabilities. At this time the representative of the helping situation, frequently the physician, must intervene to relieve distress, to foster reorganization, to identify the factors that led to this crisis, and to take steps in beginning the long-term care necessary to prevent these factors coming together again to cause future crises. However, the first aspect of rescue must be the relief of pain, pressure, and stress. Rescue is offered through environmental change, medication, and psychotherapy.

The environmental manipulation consists of altering the psychosocial space in which the individual finds himself. Stresses are relieved and support is offered. The traditional way of manipulating the environment is to hospitalize patients. We now know that many other environmental supporting techniques do as well or better than hospitalization. Alternatives to hospitalization during crisis, when they are well worked out and thoroughly studied, are more effective and less costly, and have fewer long-term side effects. When these alternatives are not available, the hospital remains a type of crisis intervention that on occasion must be used. Some of the alternatives include supporting the family and other social support systems that the patient has been able to use in the past (crisis family therapy, day treatment, social recovery services, and so forth). It may be best to remove the patient into a situation where the stress is temporarily lessened (such as putting him on vacation, taking him into the hospital, or arranging other environmental change). This intervention serves the purpose of giving his support system a temporary vacation and also gives him a chance to get out from under some of the pressures of his usual psychosocial space. There are many other direct environmental manipulations we can use. They may include having the patient join and participate in various groups (Recovery, Inc.; after-care groups; Alcoholics Anonymous; and so on). In all environmental manipulations, it is essential to make a careful assessment and identification of the specific stresses that have led to the patient's disorganization and failure of the equilibrium with his illness and with his support systems. When those pressures have been identified, then appropriate interventions can be made. These environmental manipulations must be carefully geared to the individual patient for his individual situation and must take into account the basic principle of rescue, identification of difficulties leading to crisis, training the patient for future crisis prevention, and long-term supportive care.

Any discussion of crisis intervention must include a discussion of suicide prevention. The patient must be kept alive. Generally, suicidal behavior is associated with depression. Because it is not usually associated with schizophrenia, the problem of suicide is more complicated and it is more difficult to monitor potential suicide risks. In the depressive illnesses, one can assess suicidal risk by following the depression. In the schizophrenic illnesses, however, suicidal behavior frequently cannot be predicted. Very often the patient does not appear depressed, does not talk about self-destructive attitudes, and behaves self-destructively in an almost casual way. Suicide is always a great risk in the life of the schizophrenic person. During crisis this risk is increased.

The panic a patient experiences is a frequent cause of suicide during schizophrenic crisis. This experience may be a paranoid panic in which he needs to escape from torturing and accusatory hallucinations, or it may be an attempt to escape from the emptiness, loneliness, and isolation of his schizophrenia.

The suicide attempts of schizophrenic patients tend to be

bizarre, aggressive, and unpredictable. One frequently sees the predominance of the sadistic element, that is, the wishing to kill the introject, to kill the bad, the painful, the hurting part of the self. Quite often, dying or being killed is not part of the dynamics. The major technique of suicide prevention is to offer and then maintain a human relationship. Schizophrenic patients who have an ongoing supporting relationship will not commit suicide if that relationship offers rescue and hope. The rescuing relationship, the intervention by others, the therapeutic relationship that is reliable and available is the best prevention of suicide. The relationship can penetrate the isolation and withdrawal of the patient. Placing the patient in a hospital does not prevent suicide, even though hospitalization has been a traditional practice in psychiatry. Unfortunately, patients manage to commit suicide in hospitals, too. When released from the hospital, the patient might return to a situation in which he is again able to withdraw and isolate himself and again become a candidate for suicidal behavior. If, however, during the crisis after the suicidal attempt, a therapeutic relationship can be formed that demonstrates the ability to rescue the patient and to interrupt his isolation, then the ongoingness of that relationship becomes the best prevention of suicide. Whatever is necessary must be done to prevent the suicide, because if we do not intervene successfully in that crisis we have no future opportunity for treatment.

Medication is an important therapeutic tool during crisis. Tranquilizers, when used correctly and in adequate doses, are of much help in relieving the experience of anxiety and thus producing a reorganization of personality and an opportunity for more appropriate stress management. As we mentioned in the previous chapter, there is no indication that any one of the major tranquilizers is superior to any other in terms of treating the schizophrenic crisis. The choice simply involves the side effects that are least bothersome for the particular patient. Medication must be used in adequate dosages determined by the patient's individual response. We can say that there is a range of dosages that have been found useful, but these must be adapted to the patient's needs.

Once we have decided on the use of a medication, an orderly approach must be taken to the administration of this drug, to the evaluation of the response of the patient to the drug, and to

changing either the drug or the dosage. If the patient is not responding adequately to the medication given, before a change of medication is made we should first make sure that the patient is taking the
medication. There have been estimates that up to 50 percent of
patients, even in hospitals, are not actually taking prescribed
medication. Only very skilled nursing care or proper attention by
the family members will determine whether the patient is taking
the medication. It may be necessary to give the medication in
liquid form during the acute psychotic episode to make sure that
the patient has taken it. Tests for blood levels of medication are not
terribly accurate and are not readily available in some centers, yet
on occasion they can be used to ensure proper blood level.

After we have established that the patient is taking the
medication but is not showing an adequate response, then we must
be concerned with the problem of individual variations of absorp-
tion. If there is some question about this variation, then we should
consider using intramuscular medication at appropriate levels to see
whether we can get a therapeutic response to the particular medication we are using. If we have established that the patient is taking
the medication and that he is absorbing it but not responding, then
we should increase the dosage until we get either a therapeutic
response or a major side effect. In some patients it has been found
useful to increase the medication to very high levels. If we get a
significant side effect showing that the medication is taken and
absorbed, but we are not getting a therapeutic effect, then we should
consider changing to a different tranquilizer. Perhaps in this individual at this time we will get a better therapeutic response from
another medication. There is, however, no evidence that mixing
of tranquilizers will improve therapeutic effectiveness.

In about 5 to 10 percent of patients there is a paradoxical
effect. Some psychotic persons, who are hanging on by the skin of
their teeth to reality and have tenuous control, when placed on
tranquilizers show an exacerbation of symptoms to the extent of
total disorganization of behavior and thinking and seem over-
whelmed by anxiety. This effect can be understood when we
recognize that the tranquilizer is not selective in placing a chemical
screen to decrease the awareness of anxiety. It also screens contact
with reality. Any physician using the major tranquilizers should

take at least one dose himself to have the experience of feeling that the medication produces quite apart from the effect of the schizophrenia. In those patients who have a paradoxical effect, the administration of the phenothiazine medication interrupts the tenuous hold that they have on reality and on control. They respond to the clouding of that contact with increased anxiety and internal chaos. These patients then get worse clinically. It is with such patients that we sometimes see improvement with a minor tranquilizer or even without medication.

Electroconvulsive therapy (ECT) during crisis in the treatment of the schizophrenic patient is useful in extreme situations. Generally, electroconvulsive therapy has been thoroughly discredited in the treatment of schizophrenia. During the late 1940s and 1950s, before the ready availability of the major tranquilizers, in a desperate attempt to control disorganized and difficult behavior, the psychiatric profession used electroconvulsive therapy in great excess. Many patients received 500 to 800 treatments in the course of their illness. Electroconvulsive therapy does not alter the course of schizophrenia, certainly does not cure schizophrenia, and often causes difficulties in the long-term rehabilitation of the schizophrenic patient if it is used in excessive amounts. However, on very rare occasions, we find patients suffering from schizophrenia who can benefit from a brief course of six to twelve treatments to abbreviate the crisis, to prevent suicide, or to interrupt a plateau of disorganization or nonresponse to supportive care. Electroconvulsive therapy given in the proper setting with appropriate premedication and good techniques is safe. It can be a lifesaving measure for the suicidal schizophrenic patient. It can also interrupt a crisis that is going on too long, in which a patient has not responded to medication and human intervention, and in which the disorganization seems to be following the course of illness leading to chronic psychosis. For example, ECT can be considered for severely suicidal patients who do not respond to the rescue relationship of crisis intervention or medication within two weeks.

It is important during the crisis and during rescue from the crisis that the supporting relationship help the patient to learn to use helping resources. As part of crisis intervention, we teach the patient the cause of crisis and attempt to demonstrate to him how this crisis may be related to past crises. Once the causes of past crises have been identified, then we attempt to teach the patient to arrange his life in such a way as to avoid the difficulties that led to the disorganization. Another important part of crisis intervention is to help the patient trace the initial indications he had of the oncoming crisis. For each patient this pattern may be somewhat different. Signs of early disorganization or exacerbation of problems should be cataloged with the patient, and he should learn them thoroughly, so that if at some future time the signals occur again he can more quickly reach out for help and for crisis intervention. These signs may include changes in sleep pattern, in memory, in levels of adaptation, in ability to concentrate and in appetite, as well as in increasing irritability. The signs may be first seen by others. Patients learn that if others begin to say to them they are acting strangely it is time to get help. The response of others can become a learned early warning signal of impending crisis.

The rescue from the crisis should also be used to teach the patient to arrange for any possible future rescue. He should learn how he "cried for help" this time and how he can do so in the future in the same way or even more effectively. He should learn as much as possible how to activate his rescue network, how to let the significant others know that he is in need of urgent intervention, and how to get in touch with the therapist. With some patients I have gone so far as to practice this call for help, in much the same way school children practice a fire drill. Just as the purpose of the fire drill is to make behavior automatic even in times of panic, so the purpose of practicing getting in touch with the helping resource during crisis is to make it automatic even when the patient is disorganized. We may ask him to know certain phone numbers where there will always be response (a suicide prevention center, the therapist's exchange, the community hot line, and the emergency room of a clinic or hospital). The patient and I literally practice calling these numbers. At all times the patient carries a dime taped to a card with the emergency number on it. We practice placing the phone call and giving the name and location and the appropriate request for help and intervention.

Another useful aspect of the rescue during crisis is to implant the experience concretely as a symbol of help, reifying the helping situation and making that symbol available as a symbol of help for the future. This implantation can be accomplished in many ways. It can be accomplished by reminding the patient of how he was rescued from the crisis and how this same rescue is available in the future. It can be accomplished by giving the patient a symbol of rescue such as a plastic card with his name and patient file number from the emergency center. We can give the patient a metal bracelet or a metal dog tag that bears his name, his identification number, and the number of the rescue center. The card or bracelet or dog tag may contain the statement "If I act strangely please help me to call the crisis center at Number 555-5555, so that I can get help with my illness." Such techniques of reifying rescue are useful for many patients as a reminder that help is available when needed. This reminder can do much to relieve anxiety and fear of future disorganization.

Brevity (one to five days) should be a cardinal principal of crisis intervention. If crisis care is formulated in terms of brief interventions, this approach will be both implicitly and explicitly communicated to the patient, and he will respond by preserving and fostering those of his adaptive capacities that will be important in adjusting when the crisis is over.

Crisis intervention should provide rescue for the patient, should offer relief of pain, and should be the beginning of future crisis prevention. If the crisis rescue and resolution experience has been a therapeutic one for the patient, that period of treatment can become a symbol of the helping situation and can be called on at a later date as an important link in the chain of supportive care. For some patients, the knowledge that crisis care is available, and has been part of their own treatment reality, will be sufficient to prevent future crises. The knowledge gained by working through in detail a particular crisis will give patients tools with which to prevent future crises and to predict earlier the possible onset of crisis. Still, crisis treatment is only one part of offering supportive care.

Chapter 14

❧❧❧❧❧❧❧❧

Providing Long-Term Support

Schizophrenia is, by definition, a chronic illness. Treatment requires the lifelong management of the patient and his illness. This long-term support is the backbone of the treatment of schizophrenia. Crisis intervention is required during phases of acute disorganization, periods of disturbance of the homeostasis of the patient with his psychosocial space, and periods of exacerbation of symptoms. The purpose of long-term support is to prevent or at least anticipate crises so that crisis intervention becomes less and less necessary.

The basis of long-term support is the long-term therapeutic alliance between the patient and the helping resource. This therapeutic relationship is used to help the patient with anxiety management, to guide the patient in his interpersonal relationships, and to help establish the flow of time to counteract the failure of historicity. In general, this relationship is characterized by an unending ongoingness and by the therapist's being undemanding and nonjudgmental, by providing a vehicle for rescuing the patient from situations and relationships that are beyond his emotional means (getting him off the hook), and by providing activities that keep the future open, that reinforce the therapeutic intent, and that give the patient "permission" to be different. The selective attention and inattention in the therapeutic transaction helps the patient to focus on activity, experience, and the here-and-now. It helps the patient to focus away from fantasies, delusions, and unreality, and from dwelling on the past.

The carefully controlled and carefully managed therapeutic relationship is a vehicle for alleviating the patient's distress, training him for managing his anxiety more effectively, dealing with his failure of historicity, and rescuing him from his interpersonal misadventures. It is also a quasicontrolled laboratory interpersonal relationship from which the patient can generalize to some extent out into life and from which he can be referred to other sources of support available in his psychosocial space. It is in the therapeutic relationship that the arranged experience of the therapeutic transaction teaches the patient that the relationship can be counted on, that the world can be seen as a somewhat reliable place, and that the interpersonal space may be maintained in a comfortable way without too much closeness or too much distance. From a good therapeutic experience, the patient is encouraged to reach out to life, to tap other helping and supporting resources identified by the patient and the therapist, and to learn to use these resources in a way that the patient can tolerate and that the helping resource can manage.

This description does not imply that the schizophrenic patient ever gets "well" so that he can relate normally. He continues to have the same basic disabilities. But he can learn to compensate for these disabilities so that he can have "as if" relationships. It is much the same as a physically crippled individual's learning to compensate for his defect and to function in spite of his crippling problem by using other muscles, other motions, or a prosthesis.

The need to continue some aspect of the long-term supporting relationship for the entire life of the patient creates major problems for both the patient and the therapist. The problems for the patient are those of his dependency. The problems for the therapist include the issue of countertransference in chronic supportive care and the technical problems of providing for the transfer of the patient to another therapist when transfer becomes necessary.

The management of the dependency of the patient is complex and is quite different from the management of dependency in definitive or expressive psychotherapy, where the plan is to terminate the dependency when the patient is ready. In the usual type of expressive-definitive psychotherapy, the patient enters into treatment, develops an increasingly regressive transference and dependency, and then through interpretation and transaction is helped to resolve that dependency and transference to regain his independence. The management of the increasing dependency and subsequent decreasing dependency is much of the work of expressive psychotherapy.

In providing long-term supportive care, the issues are quite different. The patient is encouraged to develop a reliance and dependency on the therapist and on the helping resource. This process is usually begun during crisis and is based on the demonstrable ability of the therapist to provide rescue, relief, and, subsequently, a plan for rehabilitation. The patient learns to accept that he is chronically ill and learns to live with certain limitations. At the same time, he must be made aware of what he can do, how he can function, and what techniques he must use to maximize his capacities. The issue of managing supportive care is essentially the issue of the titration of dependency. This issue is similar to the issue of dependency in child rearing, except that with the schizophrenic patient the rearing process never really ends. How dependent a patient should be, how much independence should be encouraged and insisted on, must be based on a thorough knowledge of the patient and on detailed clinical evaluation of his ability to function.

Inexperienced therapists err on both sides. They do not recognize changes and improvements patients have made and insist on an immobilizing dependency based on their perception of the patient's prior state of illness and disability. Other therapists, carried away by therapeutic zeal, demand an independence beyond the patient's emotional means. Such expectation and demand is also disorganizing and immobilizing to the patient. In order to manage adequately the patient's dependency and to provide the correct amount of support and the right amount of push, it is absolutely essential to make frequent evaluations of the clinical state of the patient, of his level of anxiety, and of his abilities and disabilities.

A major issue for the therapist is the recognition of the countertransference problem in providing long-term supportive care. This problem includes the very real problem of boredom. Taking care of schizophrenic patients is a very boring task. It can be carried out effectively, economically, and with satisfaction only if the clinician has an overview of the illness, the patient, and the problem. Our recognition of the effectiveness of long-term supportive care in preventing suffering and dysfunction is not enough to keep many therapists interested between crises. It is not by accident that most senior clinicians avoid providing supportive care. Usually such care is provided by the young clinician, who enjoys the discovery of his understanding of schizophrenia. But as soon as he is able, he often sends these patients to his colleagues or to social workers and concentrates his efforts on more healthy and less needy neurotic patients. Generally, only a few senior clinicians who derive satisfaction from research in the field of schizophrenia continue an interest in providing treatment for these patients. There is also a newly reemerging type of psychiatrist who gets satisfaction much like that derived by the old family physician from treating an individual and his family over an entire life span. Many of these primary-physician-type psychiatrists have an interest in providing long-term supportive care to the population of schizophrenic patients.

There is also the problem of providing long-term supportive care by one therapist when that therapist is out of town for vacation, is unavailable, or moves to another part of the country. If the therapist functions within a clinic organization, it is possible to transfer the patient to another therapist after reinforcing the therapeutic relationship with the clinic rather than with the individual therapist. Under such circumstances, many of the patients form a long-term supportive care relationship with the organization, with a particular building, or with an individual who is always there, such as a receptionist. I remember being in a clinic where the chronic schizophrenic patients were cared for by second- and third-year psychiatric residents, who changed service every six months. Patients of ten or more years standing had a new therapist every six months, but they related to the clinic and particularly to the receptionist. They were able to tolerate the changing person of the individual therapist because the personal therapist was a representative of the clinic.

Approximately fifteen years ago we attempted to clarify the best technique of changing individual therapists within the clinic setting. We compared the results of patients if we changed therapists in the traditional psychotherapeutic way of announcing the change several weeks before it occurred, if we announced the change at the last meeting before the change occurred, and if we did not announce the change at all but simply had the new therapist take over. Our results indicated that the latter two approaches were better and proved less disruptive to the patient. If the change from one therapist to another in providing long-term supportive care was announced considerably ahead of time and if the patient was expected to have feelings and problems with this change, he would.

In private practice I have developed a tandem technique that has allowed me to provide lifelong supportive care to a large group of patients without placing an undue burden on myself and without having to seem unreliable to patients at times of my vacations or personal dysfunction. This technique takes its model from the group practice of the obstetrician, by introducing the patient to alternate psychotherapists very early in the therapeutic experience. If the patient comes to me in crisis, as soon as the crisis has been resolved I will introduce him to other therapists with whom he will have several appointments. The patient will learn that the other therapists know his case well, that they subscribe to the same treatment program as the primary therapist, and that the treatment record provides continuity. He will establish a relationship with the other therapists knowing that on occasion when I am out of town for meetings or vacations, or if I am ever ill, or if I should die, the other therapists are ready to take over. When I am out of town, many of these patients have appointments with the alternate therapist or know that the alternate therapist is available if they want to see him. This tandem approach makes it feasible to provide long-term supportive care to such chronic patients and those suffering from schizophrenia in a private practice setting.

Many patients with schizophrenia must remain on medication for the rest of their lives. The evidence is that those who do better on medication should continue long after the crisis has passed. Some clinicians suggest an occasional drug holiday both to prevent the complications of long-term phenothiazine administration and to test out the possibility of the patient's getting along better without medication. It is usually recommended that this drug holiday occur once a year and extend over a period of approximately one month. The patient should be carefully watched for exacerbation of symptoms or disorganization. If these problems occur, the medications should be reinstituted earlier than the end of the month. If the patient gets along well, it is suggested that the patient might try getting along without medication.

There is some new evidence to show that after many years of requiring phenothiazines some patients get along better without them. An approach to medication management that includes an annual drug holiday would allow for such a possibility and might show that a patient who previously could not get along without regular use of phenothiazine can get along or manage better without it. We do not know how many patients do better eventually without phenothiazine or what the cause of this change is, but it has occurred frequently enough so that the phenomenon must be understood. We have accumulated forty-two such cases in our long-term supportive care population. The clinician should keep in mind that as the patient changes throughout his life the requirement for medication may differ and may eventually be abolished. He should also keep in mind that the most common cause of crises in the long-term management of schizophrenic patients is that the patient stops taking his medication. The usual course is that the patient takes the medication during crisis but discontinues as soon as he feels somewhat better. When patients receive supportive care for long periods and when this care is properly managed 75 percent are able to live their lives quite satisfactorily having appointments once a month or less frequently. Generally, 25 percent of the population may require more frequent contact to function adequately and comfortably.

The techniques of supportive care are simple to teach and learn, economically sound, and readily available. If the treatment program is organized along the lines outlined here, these techniques provide relief from pain and suffering, as well as providing markedly improved comfort and function.

Chapter 15

꙰꙰꙰꙰꙰꙰꙰

Long-Term Outcome

I am not ready to write this chapter. I do not know the long-term outcome of the lives of schizophrenic persons. In another thirty years, at the end of my career, when I have had the opportunity to live with my population of schizophrenic patients through their middle age and into old age, I will have the rest of the observations I need.

Most of the patients whom I have followed for twenty years are now in their early or late forties. I have much information about how they came into treatment, what their crises were in adolescence and in early adulthood, how they survived getting married or not

121

getting married, what they did about graduating and going to work, how they handled success and failure, and how they handled divorce, financial reverses, wealth, and power. I have lived with 500 patients from ages twenty to forty. During that time I have gotten to know them well and have learned to identify their problems in living. I have collected the history of how schizophrenia affects the lives of people when they are not institutionalized, when the illness is not complicated by the side effects of chronic enforced alienation from society through chronic hospitalization. In order to write this chapter, however, I need the information about the second half of their lives. I have treated older schizophrenic people and I have known older patients socially. These individuals were in their fifties, sixties, and seventies. They continued to display the three nuclear clusters of disabilities in the area of anxiety management, interpersonal relationship, and failure of historicity. They showed a tangentiality and an apartheid that are typical of living life with schizophrenia. Tentativeness in decisions and interpersonal relationships was always identifiable. Because I had not known them in their younger days, in the days of their "hot" schizophrenia, but knew them only in their "burned out" stage, and because many of them had had prolonged hospitalization, I do not feel that I can use that cross-sectional and skimpy knowledge as a basis for understanding life with schizophrenia after forty. I need to follow my population for the next thirty years in order to have that information.

The older literature offers some information about the long-term outcome of schizophrenia. These observations are adulterated by the patients' long hospitalization. When I first came into psychiatry, before the days of tranquilizers and treatment in the community, I worked in hospitals where many patients had been kept for twenty, thirty, and forty years. As a first-year resident at St. Elizabeth's Hospital in Washington, D.C., where 7,000 mentally ill individuals were cared for over long periods, I remember there were patients who had been there continuously for sixty years. These patients were clearly identifiable, being "burned out," withdrawn, idiosyncratic in their behavior, silly in their affect, with tight paranoid systems related to the state of the world at the time of their initial psychotic disorganization. All we saw was the result of prolonged chronic hospitalization, of fifty years of living in a psychotic world of the large, tightly organized community of a government hospital apart from the real world.

In the post-World War II literature, there are many examples of patients who went to state hospitals incorrectly diagnosed either as schizophrenic or as mentally retarded and who then stayed for thirty or forty years only to be discovered, during the renaissance of psychiatry after World War II, not to be ill at all. These patients show a psychological condition based entirely on having been in the hospital for thirty or forty years without any initial mental illness or mental retardation. Since many of these patients were as incapacitated as anyone who had been ill all of his life, we cannot use such observations as a vehicle for understanding the long-term outcome of schizophrenia. We are now gathering data and following patients who have not been hospitalized for extensive periods, who have been maintained with supportive care in the community. By 1990 we will know what happens to them in the last two or three decades of their lives.

Up to now, after twenty years of observation, I can report on the long-term outcome for some 479 chronic schizophrenia patients. Of these patients, 75 percent were able to manage their lives between crises quite satisfactorily with minimal support of once a month or less frequently. The other 25 percent of the population required more frequent contact in order to function adequately and comfortably. Generally, crises occurred more frequently in the first decade of the illness, during which the patient dealt with the storms and stresses of biological growth, sexuality, role identification, marriage, having children, losing parents, becoming adults, graduating, and entering an occupation or profession. Many of my patients spent no time in the hospital even during the most severe crises; all of the problems could be handled in an outpatient setting, in a day-care center, in the home, in a social recovery station, or with intensive contact in the office, by mobilizing social support in the community, the family, and their circle of acquaintances. Others spent two or three days in the hospital, between one and three times in their lives. Each time, the hospitalization was a result not of their illness but of the disorganization of support forces, or an inability on my part to muster the necessary resources of caring for the patient at the very moment when he needed it, or my need for a brief vacation. (Certainly the long-term care of chronic schizophrenic patients makes it clear that hospitalization is an expensive, inadequate way of providing crisis treatment. The many side effects must be dealt with afterwards and complicate the life of the schizophrenic person. All of the services that we traditionally provide in the hospital can be better provided, less expensively, and with fewer side effects in other kinds of settings. The only reason we continue to use the hospitals as centers for crisis intervention is because they are there. Thus suitable alternatives have not been developed in many communities.)

Just as Thomas Sydenham (1624–1689) said to his students hundreds of years ago, "Gentlemen, throw away your books and go back to the bedside," I would like to propose that we close this unfinished chapter on long-term outcome by sketching two typical case histories of patients who have lived their lives with schizophrenia between the ages of twenty and forty.

Case History: George Fine

George Fine, who is now a single, thirty-four-year-old accountant, first came to my attention in 1959 at the age of eighteen. At that time he had dropped out of high school in his junior year and was involved in serious conflicts with both of his parents. Three years earlier his parents had been divorced. His father, an attorney, was an alcoholic. His mother had had several periods of serious depressions and suicide attempts. He was the oldest of three siblings. One brother two years younger had run away from home several times, stolen cars, and ended up in juvenile hall. Another brother, four years younger than George, was diagnosed as schizophrenic and had been permanently in a state hospital since the age of twelve. The family was broken up by the divorce and George went to live with his father, who still functioned adequately as an attorney. He had provided a roof for George but little parental supervision.

When George first came to me, he showed symptoms of a major psychosis. He had developed severe obsessional symptoms approximately one year prior to the 1959 crisis. These symptoms consisted of washing compulsions that required him to spend three hours each morning showering and shaving, compulsions in which he needed to repeat over and over again certain key religious phrases ("Hear, O Israel," "The Lord Our God," "The Lord is One"). He needed to say these phrases twenty-seven times in the morning and then six times each hour. He said the phrases both in Hebrew and in English, and if he did not pronounce the words perfectly he would have to say them over and over again. This incapacitating compulsive state continued for approximately one year and could be relieved only by the use of medication. At that time he was using some phenobarbital, some alcohol, and some Thorazine prescribed by the family physician.

At the age of eighteen, just prior to coming for his first serious psychiatric treatment, he began hearing accusatory voices, felt that he was homosexual and looked like a queer, and became increasingly stiff and rigid in his physical movements. He would spend most of the day sitting in his room. On two or three occasions he had major outbursts of anger during which he punched his fist through the wall or broke the glass shower door. When I met George in the emergency room, he had made a suicide attempt with an overdose of barbiturates but had been found by his father.

I began the crisis intervention with a series of interviews with his father and mother. I prescribed medication and placed George on the medical ward of the general hospital in the community in which he lived. For a period of three or four days I sedated him and began treatment with chlorpromazine in the therapeutic doses (200 mg/q.i.d.). I began regular psychotherapy appointments with him in the hospital and continued them on a two-times-a-week basis as soon as he left the hospital. I made arrangements for him to live in a guest house that was primarily for young adults who were working. This guest house provided individual rooms and one meal a day with the other boarders. During the day everyone in the guest house worked on a job and during the evening there were some opportunities for socializing, although no organized program was set up except on special occasions such as holidays. I made arrangements with an occupational therapist to meet with the patient once a week to help him to plan his personal life, including budgeting the allowance he received from his father, planning for leisure activities, and thinking about a career and a job. I required that the patient engage in at least one social activity a week whether he wanted to or not, whether he found it enjoyable or not. The social activity was like medicine, it was something that had to be done and was part of the treatment program. He would plan the activity (such as going to a public dance, going to a ski meeting, going to a Young Democrats discussion, or whatever)' with the occupational therapist, and he talked to me about what happened each time. These required social contacts were major demands on him, resulting in much discomfort and many crisis telephone calls in the middle of the night. However, my firm insistence that he must go forth and report back to me had the effect of setting up a pattern of going into one new social event each week. I also required of him that twice a day he go out of his room and take a walk in the neighborhood for at least one hour. He had to report to me about these walks. Within a couple of months I required of him that he talk to at least one stranger during the walk. It did not matter what he said to them; it could be asking for the time of the day, it could be saying hello, it could be borrowing a match. Over the next two years he developed some techniques of interacting beyond these clumsy beginnings. I also required of him that he keep his appointments with me on a regular basis and on time, that he live within his budget, and that he keep his appointments with the occupational therapist. This program was all that was required. Within this setting the supportive care was provided.

During the first two years there were many midnight phone calls from George threatening to commit suicide, wanting me to give him reasons why he should not kill himself, why he should continue living. There were many panic calls when he told me that he could not go on, that he could not do what I asked of him. There were specific social crises when he was rejected by the people he tried to talk to. On one occasion he was arrested in a grocery store on suspicion of shoplifting. In each of these situations I intervened quickly and effectively. I, or my tandem therapist, was always available for rescue. Many times I would go out in the middle of the night to his apartment and sit with him for an hour or two while he talked obsessively about committing suicide. At no time did I offer him hospitalization. Toward the end of the second year of treatment he demanded to be hospitalized in the psychiatric hospital because he felt he could not go on in the pain and agony, the loneliness and discomfort of his existence. I tried to talk him out of it, but he mobilized his father into demanding hospitalization. I referred him to a local private psychiatric hospital and told him that he could be admitted there but I did not recommend it. He and his father went over to the hospital, where he remained for six hours. When he saw what the hospital was like, he demanded to leave. I accepted him back into the prior treatment situation.

Even though it was not continuously obvious, over the first two years it became clear that he was able to function much better, that his obsessions were receding, and that his major psychotic symptoms had disappeared. He was no longer hearing voices. Although his self-esteem was still impaired, he did not believe that he was homosexual. He even began making some clumsy attempts at finding new friends. Usually these friendships and acquaintances were with people whom he met in his boardinghouse or on his walks and who reached out to him. Quite apart from his many emotional problems, he was a very gentle person who was rather good-looking and very bright. At the end of the two years, with the prodding of the occupational therapist, he decided to go to a continuation high school and get his diploma. He successfully completed that task after severe failures and after dropping the effort four times, and graduated from high school at the age of twenty-one. His contact with his family (at my encouragement) was limited to a visit once a month to his father and once a month to his mother. Both of them had remarried to spouses of whom the patient disapproved and of whom he was jealous. He also visited his youngest hospitalized brother approximately once every six months but had no contact with his other brother, who was by then in the state reformatory. His contact with me by this time was on a once-a-week basis, except during minor crises. In 1962, at the age of twenty-one, he made a very clumsy attempt at a relationship with a girl. He tried to become sexually involved and was rejected. His response was a severe withdrawal and forty-eight hours of a return of his obsessive compulsive symptoms. He sat in his room without eating or sleeping for several days before I was called by the housemother of the guesthouse. Since he was now one of the oldest tenants, she had taken a considerable interest in him and knew something about his psychotic difficulties. During this crisis he temporarily moved into his father's new home with his stepmother, where he remained for approximately two weeks. He again developed hallucinations and delusions, although in this crisis there was no evidence of suicidal ideation. However, more than ever before he showed evidence of a major thought process disorder and began to develop some negativism toward me as well as some paranoid delusions—that I was experimenting with him and that I was really just trying to torture him because I hated him. After approximately two weeks he began pulling together, was able to move back into the guesthouse, and seemed to go to a level of integration that was higher than before this last break. We went back to weekly psychotherapy and he continued his phenothiazine medication on a regular basis. He began thinking about his future and was able to take a part-time job in a hamburger stand for four hours a day. Apparently he did quite well, since he stayed on for several years even after he started college.

In 1962, at the age of twenty-two, George was holding a part-time job, had a circle of "friends" with whom he had very tenuous relationships but on whom he could call to interrupt his isolated loneliness. He had also developed a stable relationship with both of his parents, interrupted by regular crises every three or four months, usually about his need for extra money. He now was ready to consider going to college. He had no career in mind, although he was quite certain that he did not want to follow in his father's footsteps, feeling that he could never get into law school and could never be an attorney. He and I decided to evaluate his potential for a career and to explore all of his interests in a very orderly way. In the meantime, he thought he might get started in college and he enrolled in three courses, English, Spanish, and psychology, at a local junior college. His major difficulty in going to college was his concern with the social interactions in the classroom. He was again afraid that others might look at him and that he would appear as strange or different. Though he was no longer concerned with the issue of homosexuality, he had not yet made a satisfactory heterosexual relationship. His sexual contacts had been limited to several arranged by his friends with local prostitutes.

In school he found it difficult to concentrate, to understand what the teachers wanted. In the first semester he dropped two of his three courses. English he completed successfully with a grade of B, by which he was very much encouraged. This success was not accomplished without feelings of hopelessness, several crises during the middle of the night, and wondering why he was going through all of this.

The details of the next few years were a continuation of slow progress. There were many minor crises that lasted two or three days but that never required more than an extra appointment or some adjustment in medication. There were no further suicide attempts, although there was considerable thought on his part about whether life was worth it. By 1965, at the age of twenty-four, George had enough grades together to get himself into the local state college. With the assistance of considerable testing and self-searching, he decided that he would become a bookkeeper or accountant. He liked math, though he wondered if he had any real talent. In 1968, at the age of twenty-seven, he graduated from college as a business administration major with a C + average. In his last year in college he had managed several dates with girls, none of which led to a long-term relationship. His sexual contacts were still limited to prostitutes except for one occasion when he became sexually involved with a drunk girl at a college party, after which he had a severe anxiety attack wondering how he would face her in school during the next days. When the girl seemed to act as though nothing had happened, he was devastated and ruminated for months about the inadequacy of his sexual performance.

During this last year of college he changed part-time jobs. He worked as a parking attendant at various restaurants and subsequently worked for one of the part-time help agencies going out as a temporary bookkeeper. In the process he began to make enough money to almost support himself and his car. During his last year in college our therapeutic contacts were limited to a once-a-month visit, though we had phone contact once a week in which he would call to pass the time or ask advice. He was using me more and more as a friend. The phone calls would come often on Saturday or Sunday nights, when he was not working and had no place to go and felt bored and isolated and different from everyone else. I would chat with him for ten or fifteen minutes about such things as movies he had seen or movies I had seen, about plans for the next vacation, and so forth. It was also during this period that we began moving our contact more and more into the social sphere. I would get together with him every few weeks for lunch and I invited him to my home for dinner. We continued seeing each other once a month for a therapy appointment. In the appointment we concentrated on managing his medication and on identifying the kinds of problems that were causing him major difficulty. We also reviewed the signals of disorganization for which he could watch.

In 1970, at the age of twenty-nine, after graduation from the state college, he entered a local private business school to learn accounting. Since the tuition was fairly high, he had to ask his father for some help with money. This request again became a major focus of difficulty between the two of them. The father used the money to try to control George. George again felt helpless and dependent. It was during the first few weeks of this school experience, either because of the new demands made on George or because of the new relationship with his father, that he began disorganizing. For approximately two weeks he again became concerned about being a homosexual, he heard voices accusing him of being queer, and he thought the other students looked at him peculiarly.

During those two weeks I increased my contact with him to two times per week and increased his medication. He and I explored the stresses at that moment in his life. We were able to recognize his problems as symptoms of increased pressure. We dealt with these directly. We had a joint meeting with his father to discuss how the money could be handled in a better way for George. The father agreed to immediately deposit a total of $1,000 in George's account so that he could have it available to complete his studies without asking over the next year and a half. In this way George was somewhat unhooked from the difficult relationship with the father. George and I explored in detail the difficulties in the new college, particularly his need to relate to a new set of people who seemed to be a more adult group than he had been used to. We practiced talking to adult fellow students and explored the kinds of relationships he would have with these people, and he understood that even though it was called a *college* it was in fact an adult school for people entering careers. During the first semester he performed poorly and began to develop some obsessive symptoms. For the first time he found it difficult to study. He was spending too much time ruminating about what he should or should not study, and how many hours he should spend on homework and on his part-time jobs. He began making lists and remaking these lists. This compulsion became incapacitating for him to the extent that he had no time for anything else. As we looked at the details of his symptoms and explored them as signs and symptoms of his anxiety, he began giving them up.

In 1972 he graduated. He obtained a job as a public accountant with a large firm. Again he had major difficulties in the job interview. We practiced job interview behavior extensively to prepare him for this ordeal. Since he had been recommended by the college, the firm decided to hire him even though George felt he had been essentially nonfunctional during the interview. On the job he felt terribly uncomfortable and peculiar. He was very uncomfortable with the females at work, and when a secretary was friendly with him, apparently interested in setting up a social relationship with him that would include dating, he became so confused that he had to go home for the rest of the day. Since he had not yet been able to form a comfortable heterosexual relationship, and always felt terribly embarrassed by his heterosexual misadventures, I suggested that he should not become socially or sexually involved with the people at work. I did encourage him to seek the experience and practice of social and sexual relationships in another setting. We again made a list of the organizations and clubs representing various activities ranging from skiing to hiking to conservation groups where he might meet people.

In 1976 he is thirty-five years old, single and still terribly uncomfortable socially. During recent months he dated a girl six times in a row. He is supporting himself, taking his medication, and keeping a monthly appointment with me. He has a pleasant furnished bachelor apartment in a house devoted to single adults. He has some social life, although he is always at the periphery. His disabilities in the area of anxiety management and in the area of interpersonal relationships continue to be clearly evident. His failure of historicity appears in each crisis in his life when he faces a new situation or a new relationship as though it were the first time. If he cannot reach me by phone on the same day, by the next day he often acts as though he has entirely given up our long-standing relationship.

Case History: Ellen East

Ellen East was a senior student at a major university when I first met her in 1960. At that time she was twenty-two years old. She was referred to me by the student health service after a major psychotic episode that seemed to have been precipitated following a general sepsis that was presumed to be secondary to a nonmedical abortion. When the patient was referred to me, her history stated that there had been no prior mental illness.

Ellen was born in Springfield, Ohio, as the youngest of three girls, one sister being four years older and another sister two years older. Her father was a wholesale grocer. She had lived all of her life in the comfortable middle-class surroundings of Springfield until she came to the West Coast to attend college. Her major interest all her life had been in gadgets, electricity, and engineering. She had come to the university to become an engineer.

At the time I first encountered the patient she appeared grossly psychotic. Her mental status examination demonstrated delusions. She had the idea that electricity was being passed through her body, that her thoughts were controlled by radio waves, and that there was a group of people from New York who were trying to steal her "great invention." It was not quite clear what the great invention was, but it involved a new way of sending radio waves for long distances. She experienced auditory hallucinations in which she overheard male voices planning the theft of her idea. She showed no evidence of a toxic condition nor did I find anything consistent with organic impairment.

A more detailed history from her parents, who had flown out at the time of crisis, and her former husband (although they were in the midst of a divorce, he was still willing to participate in the evaluation of the patient) revealed that there had been previous psychiatric problems. The parents described Ellen as rather different

from her sisters and as very seclusive all of her life. She never had
friends in school, stayed by herself, tended to be characterized as the
"strange genius" in the family, and was emotionally labile. Her
parents reported that at age sixteen she had had a "personality
change," which to them meant that she became disobedient, argu-
mentative, stubborn, and, according to the mother, sexually pro-
miscuous. Her parents described the patient as very popular in
spite of her seclusiveness because she had always been good-looking
and very bright. At age eighteen the patient had a severe case of
hepatitis, for which she was hospitalized for several weeks. She also
stayed in bed several more weeks at home after discharge from the
hospital. As a result of her "hepatitis," she missed her high school
graduation. During the period of hepatitis her parents felt she was
acting very strangely; they thought that this behavior was caused
by her physical condition. However, after recovering from the
illness she seemed stranger than she had ever been before.

In the fall she went to California to enroll in the university.
She had chosen California because she had an uncle who lived there
and who was willing to look in on her once in a while. Going to
college gave her the opportunity to get away from home. After two
years she married a senior engineering student at the university.

The relationship was a very shallow one right from the beginning. My interview revealed that neither husband nor wife
knew the other very well. Their initial attraction was sexual, but
even in that arena their contact was not satisfying to either. Soon
after the marriage (the parents of the patient strongly disapproved
because the husband was Jewish) the patient became pregnant.
Neither wanted children, so they arranged for her to have an abortion in Tijuana. There were no medical complications. After the
abortion Ellen started drinking heavily and seemed very strange in
many ways. She was also frequently sexually involved with a number
of men in a casual way.

At the time of my first contact with Ellen she had again
become pregnant and had again gone to Tijuana to have a second
abortion. This time she developed medical complications, including
a high fever for which she was treated at the student health service.
She confessed her nonmedical abortion to the health service per-
sonnel because she was afraid of dying. She responded well to

antibiotics and proper medical management, but she became grossly psychotic when the medical symptoms cleared up.

During the first two weeks of contact with me, I saw her daily on the medical ward of the student health service. I met with her husband and I also met with her parents, who had been called by the husband to come out during the crisis. The patient was placed on Stelazine, a therapeutic relationship was formed during the rescue, and the task of long-term supportive care was begun. Psychiatric examination revealed that the patient had been hearing voices and having delusions continuously for approximately six years. She had been able to hide this difficulty from her parents, her husband, and her associates because she was very bright. She had been able to hide some of her more bizarre symptoms because she was generally accepted in the role of being a "genius" because of her unusual interest in engineering, circuits, and electronics. She played the role of genius with her family and her friends. In spite of her high IQ, her performance in college had been irregular. In 1960, at the age of twenty-two and a senior in college, her grade point average was at a $C +$ level. There were courses in which she had been able to get A's but she had a number of D's as well. Apparently her performance was related to her intermittent ability to concentrate, a disability related to the stresses she was experiencing in her life. In her sophomore year she had a straight A semester. Since her marriage at the end of the sophomore year, her performance had been worse.

After two weeks of hospitalization in the general medical ward of the student health service, the patient pulled together. She was less disorganized and the intensity of her auditory hallucinations decreased. Her parents interpreted her illness as resulting from the trauma of the impending divorce and the postabortion infection. They were not able to recognize that she had had serious psychiatric problems most of her life, and they were quite defensive about admitting to prior problems.

So that the patient could finish her work toward a degree during the next three months, it was decided that the mother would move in with Ellen. It was an uncomfortable situation for the patient, but it was the only way in which she could obtain the necessary support and the interruption of her isolation from loneliness. I also felt that this ongoing contact with someone was necessary to forestall any possible suicidal behavior, and that it would serve the purpose of motivating her to once again get on her feet and become independent. She was motivated to get away from her mother. By the end of the school year she had much improved, her symptoms were under excellent control, and she was able to participate in the graduation. She spent a good deal of time studying for finals and was able to manage them very well, getting excellent grades. Her father came out from Springfield and the patient had much gratification going through the graduation ceremony, even though she pooh-poohed it and said she was only doing it "for my parents."

After her graduation, when the divorce was final, the patient had no further contact with her exhusband. Her parents left for an around-the-world trip and the patient started looking for work. She had a great deal of anxiety while looking for a job. The college provided leads and she went for interviews. After several weeks of searching, she was hired by the local department of water and power for a low-level engineering job. Her major anxiety was about her ability to perform and her ability to relate to others in the office. She felt that they would all soon learn that she was "crazy." However, her job went quite well and her performance was satisfactory.

Within two months, one of the younger engineers began dating her and they became sexually involved. Others were interested in her in the office and she found it totally impossible to deal with the situation. She was dating several of them but found the social interaction so complex that she handled her anxiety by staying home, going to bed, and calling in sick. This crisis continued for several days during which I saw her and tried to encourage her to get going and to go back to work. She wanted to quit her job, simply not to face the situation again. I put considerable pressure on her not to quit, since it was a good job that she enjoyed. Although she agreed to go back to work, the night of that appointment she made a suicide attempt by taking an overdose of tranquilizers. She called me immediately after she had taken the medication and I rushed to her apartment and took her to the local general hospital to get her stomach pumped out. I spent the rest of the night sitting up with her at my house while she had angry and very paranoid outbursts. She felt that I was trying to steal her personality, to kill her, to keep her enslaved in a job she hated. She berated me for keeping her alive and insisted she had the right to die. She said that she felt like agitated hamburger distributed throughout the universe, and she characterized my efforts to pull her together as painful and not called for. By morning I seriously considered the need for hospitalization, but she seemed to calm down enough to accompany me to my office at the university. I had her spend most of the day there, seeing her intermittently between my various duties. By evening she seemed to pull together enough to be able to go home to her apartment. I called her three or four times during the evening and set up an appointment for the following day. Within two days she seemed to be again in an excellent period of remission and to have no further difficulty. She did quit the job and was unemployed for a period of three months. She went on various interviews, but each time she became frightened about a possible social interaction. Eventually she decided not to work in engineering. This decision was not because she was not good at it, but because she wanted to avoid the "office complexities." She took a job as a waitress in a local diner in which she lasted half a day. She was so anxious about remembering the orders that after fighting her anxiety for four hours she walked off the job, saying she was sick and would not be back.

Next she took a position as a clerk with an insurance company, again facing the difficulties of a large office but remaining aloof and apart from everyone. On this job she lasted for six months before she was willing to try another engineering job. Subsequently, she again applied to the department of water and power. They were willing to take her back. For the next three years she worked regularly at that job, receiving several pay raises, but carefully avoiding any promotions. She had no social contact with anyone at the office. She was generally considered snobbish and aloof by her fellow workers. In the evenings, at my considerable prodding, she made an effort to go out at least once a week to some organization. She felt she was not able to go on dates, that she could not define her sexual interaction adequately, and that it was best for her to avoid all one-to-one contact with men or friends. Her weekly activities consisted of taking courses in the college extension division on various subjects unrelated to her profession, joining art groups, and participating in local small theater groups. In the course of her participation in an art group she met her second husband, a young physician whom she dated for approximately six months prior to considering marriage. This young physician came to see me at the patient's request and the three of us discussed her situation, her background, and her difficulty. He continued to be interested in having her as a wife and the wedding date was set. At the time of her second marriage (his first), the patient was thirty years old. After the wedding the patient terminated her employment and helped her· husband in his office for several months. She began having considerable difficulty with his demands for intimacy. Sexually the adjustment was excellent, but his other demands for closeness and sharing made her feel inadequate, queer, helpless, and hopeless. During the first few months of her marriage, I saw her for an appointment only once every three months, but within a year she was having an exacerbation of her symptoms, including the development of many somatic complaints. These complaints consisted of fear of dying, fear of heart attacks, and generalized upper gastrointestinal pain. She was thoroughly evaluated from a medical point of view and no organic basis for her pathology was found. She had continued with her phenothiazine although the dosage had been lowered to 5 mg of Stelazine daily. Her index of disorganization was always sleep pattern disturbance. When she could not sleep for several days, or when she was awakened by vivid nightmares, she knew that things were going wrong and learned to call for help.

I began seeing her on a regular once-a-week basis again and she seemed to calm down very quickly. She became pregnant, although this event was not planned. She and I talked about the possible consequences of having the constant responsibility of a child. We discussed this problem in some considerable detail for several sessions in the husband's presence. In spite of my concerns and reminders that therapeutic abortions were readily available, she and her husband decided to carry the pregnancy to term. Her life course in the last trimester was excellent and she seemed to improve, showing no evidence of any psychotic symptoms. She gave birth to a healthy girl, and handled the birth beautifully (with her visiting mother's assistance) and without any psychiatric difficulty.

There was no hint of postpartum psychosis, and for the next year she functioned with minimal contact with me and apparently maximal satisfaction in tending to the child.

After a year it was discovered that the child had a minor congenital heart problem. She took the child to various physicians, who advised that the child should be watched but that nothing needed to be done at the moment and that probably she would grow out of it. However, the patient tremendously exaggerated the difficulty. She called me frequently in tears, and became disorganized within three days after the diagnosis had been made. She accused herself of being a bad mother and of passing on defective genes, and she developed major psychotic symptoms. She heard accusatory voices and became delusional about her husband wanting to kill her and the child, mixed with ideas that she herself would kill the child to save it from a life of heart disease. She entertained suicidal ideas, called me many times a day, and was unable to cope with her home situation. The husband's sister, who was a nurse, came into the home to help with the child. The patient's medication was increased and she had daily contact with me. Hospitalization was seriously considered, but we decided the patient should go back to Ohio to visit with her parents until she felt better. As these plans were being made, the patient became very frightened by suicidal ideas, called the suicide prevention center, and was referred to me. This crisis occurred during the Christmas season and apparently I was unable to respond massively enough, since I was concerned with my personal affairs. After very careful consideration, and consultation with my tandem therapist and with my family (we were planning to go away for a week of skiing between Christmas and New Year's) I decided to hospitalize the patient. Quite frankly, and with the full knowledge of the patient and her husband, this hospitalization was undertaken because of my wish to go away on vacation. The patient was happy to accept the hospitalization and entered the local psychiatric hospital. She remained there for a week, receiving phenothiazine and participating in the milieu.

When I returned from my vacation after one week, she was released from the hospital, seemed to have pulled together quite well, and was able to return to her home, where her sister-in-law was still functioning in caring for the child. During subsequent weeks the patient improved to the point of being asymptomatic. In psychotherapy with me, she dealt with her overwhelming feelings of inadequacy as a mother and returned to a stage of remission that was every bit as good as in the previous year.

In the following year, she and her husband discussed the possibility of another pregnancy with me, since they did not want to rear an only child. I again raised serious questions about her ability to handle two children, reminded them of the difficulty she had had, and suggested that perhaps a second child might not be the best thing. In spite of this advice, they decided to go ahead. They had another daughter, and again there were no major problems in the postpartum period.

The patient is now thirty-seven years old. I see her once a month. She continues on low-dosage phenothiazine. During the past two years she has continued to be plagued by feelings of inadequacy as a wife and mother, but she can talk about these feelings and has not shown any evidence of psychotic disorganization. Her major difficulty is structuring her life with her husband and her children in such a way that she has some time for herself. She misinterprets much of her husband's and children's activities as demands on her for performance at higher levels of function. She clearly shows all three of the major disabilities of schizophrenia, yet she is asymptomatic for psychotic symptoms.

Postscript. These two abbreviated case histories serve well to paint the picture of lives lived with schizophrenia. Neither one of these patients had the course of schizophrenia complicated by prolonged hospitalization. Neither had their lives subjected to social and economic chaos caused by lower-class status in the middle-class majority culture. Both patients are Caucasian, American-born, and comfortably embedded in their middle-class environment. Their difficulties in conducting their lives are entirely the result of their illness and the consequent discomfort, dysfunction, and disability.

Annotated Bibliography

Chapter 1

BINSWANGER, L. "The Case of Ellen West." In R. May, E. Angel, and H. Ellenberger (Eds.), *Existence*. New York: Basic Books, 1958.

Binswanger was the leader of European existential psychiatry. In this article, he demonstrates his emphasis on exploring in detail the world of the individual who lives with schizophrenia and on using these observations as a basis for understanding the illness. This case is his most famous, widely quoted throughout the world literature. I translated this work from German into English for inclusion in this volume. The translation took me several years and it is from this process of translation that I first learned to understand and use the existential approach to psychopathology.

FOUCAULT, M. *Madness and Civilization.* New York: Pantheon Books, 1965.

This book presents a thoughtful social history of the role of insanity in civilization. The author recognizes that the mad-man, like the leper, has a specific function to fulfill in society.

SZASZ, T. *The Myth of Mental Illness.* New York: Harper & Row, 1963.

In this work, the author summarizes his critique of the concept of mental illness. He presents a logical argument for not using the concept of illness. He points to logical errors that are implied in the concept of mental illness and he points to the excesses of treatment that result from such errors.

Chapter 2

CARPENTER, W., STRAUSS, J., AND MULEH, S. "Are There Pathog-nomanic Symptoms in Schizophrenia?" *Archives of General Psychiatry,* 1973, *28,* 847–852.

Throughout the literature, there are attempts at describ-ing symptoms that are considered pathognomanic in schizo-phrenia. Such lists have been learned by students for several generations. Yet, when these lists are applied to the under-standing of a specific case into the making of a diagnosis, many difficulties ensue, which are discussed by the authors.

MELLOR, C. "First Rank Symptoms of Schizophrenia." *British Journal of Psychiatry,* 1970, *117,* 15–23.

In this excellent summary, the author discusses Kurt Schneider's system of first- and second-rank symptoms of schizo-phrenia. Subsequent work has shown that considerable diffi-culties are encountered when these lists of symptoms are applied in other countries, other cultures, and to other social classes.

PARFITT, D. "The Neurology of Schizophrenia." *Journal of Mental Science,* 1956, *102,* 671–718.

The title of this paper is a misnomer. Rather, it is an excellent description of the natural history of schizophrenia prior to the wide use of modern antipsychotic medication. In this article, the author presents a very accurate description of the course of schizophrenia when it is essentially left untreated.

PAYNE, R. "Disorders of Thinking." In C. G. Costello (Ed.), *Symptoms of Psychopathology: A Handbook*. New York: John Wiley & Sons, 1970.

Much has been made of the primacy of the thought disorder in schizophrenia. In this article the author reviews the evidence for the thought process disorder in schizophrenia and compares this disorder to other types of disorders of thinking.

Chapter 3

BROWN, N. *Life Against Death*. New York: Vintage Books, 1959.

In this superb book, the author who is a psychoanalytically trained historian reviews human history in terms of man's struggle against anxiety. It is fascinating to review the problem of anxiety against the panorama of recorded history.

ERIKSON, E. *Childhood and Society*. New York: W. W. Norton, 1950.

This well-known book by Erik Erikson, who is a child analyst and psychoanalytic theoretician, summarizes a point of view that looks at the road to maturity in terms of changing patterns of trust.

FREUD, A. *The Ego and the Mechanisms of Defense*. New York: International Universities Press, 1946.

In this small volume, Freud's daughter presents the fundamentals of ego psychology. Since 1946, much work and many books have appeared that further these ideas. However, this simple, small book remains the best description of the psychoanalytic concept of anxiety management.

Chapter 4

CHODOFF, P. "The German Concentration Camp as a Psychological Stress." *Archives of General Psychiatry*, 1970, 22, 78–87.

A number of articles in the recent literature attempt to describe what happened to human beings under conditions of overwhelming stress in the German concentration camps. These conditions gave rise to a major rupture of faith of a human being in his fellow man. The outcome for many was a lifelong disability that was not unrelated to schizophrenia, yet that was always clearly distinguishable from schizophrenia.

JASPERS, K. *General Psychopathology*. (J. Hoenig and M. Hamilton, Trans.) Chicago: University of Chicago Press, 1963.

Jaspers is a psychiatrist, a phenomenologist, and, more recently, a philosopher. In this book he demonstrates a clear phenomenological approach to description and understanding of psychopathology. He presents here the best example of German phenomenology as distinct from the Swiss Daseinsanalyse (existential analysis).

SEARLES, H. "Transference Psychosis in the Psychotherapy of Schizophrenia." *International Journal of Psychoanalysis*, 1963, *44*, 249–281.   •

Searles, in this paper and in his life's work, represents the psychoanalytic approach to the treatment of schizophrenia. All treatment of schizophrenia requires the management of interpersonal relationships, first in the treatment transaction and then in life. This management can be accomplished from a variety of viewpoints; Searles approaches it psychoanalytically.

WYNNE, L. "Communication Disorders and the Quest for Relatedness in Families of Schizophrenics." In R. Cancro (Ed.), *Annual Review of the Schizophrenia Syndrome*. Vol. 2. New York: Brunner/Mazel, 1972.

This contribution is an excellent example of the series of articles that have appeared in the recent literature. This article, and others like it, offer excellent observations and descriptions of the specific problems in communication between individuals who live with schizophrenia and their fellow family members.

Chapter 5

BINSWANGER, L. "Symptom und Zeit." *Schweizerische Medizinische Wochenschrift*, 1951, *81*, 510–512.

In this brief article, Binswanger looks at the distortions in the experience of lived time occurring in various states of psychopathology and relates these distortions to symptom formation. The problems of historicity that the schizophrenic patient • experiences are very much related to the differences in the experience of time.

HEIDEGGER, M. "Sein und Zeit." *Jahrbuch für Philosophie und Phenomenologische Forschung*, 1927, *8*, 1–438.

German phenomenology, which is a precursor of existential psychiatry, is based on the work of three major philosophers: Brentano, Husserl, and Heidegger. In this work, Martin Heidegger describes a philosophy based on relating the experience of time to existence. This monumental work is the basis of our understanding of the phenomenology of time.

LANZKRON, J., AND WOLFSON, W. "Prognostic Value of Perceptual Distortion of Temporal Disorientation in Chronic Schizophrenia." *American Journal of Psychiatry*, 1958, *114*, 744–746.

The authors attempt to use their understanding of the perceptual distortion of time in patients with schizophrenia. They relate such distortions to prognosis. However, they are concerned primarily with temporal disorientation rather than with the experience of the passage of time.

MINKOWSKI, E. *Le Temps vécu.* Paris: Collection de l'Evolution Psychiatrique, 1933.

Minkowski was the founder and leader of the French school of categorical phenomenology. He focuses on the experience of time and emphasizes the differences between various categories of time experience. His approach to understanding time is also an approach to understanding psychopathology.

SCHILDER, P. "Psychopathology of Time." *Journal of Nervous and Mental Disease*, 1936, *83*, 530–546.

This article, an early paper by one of the important thinkers in psychiatry, relates experience of perception of time to various states of psychopathology.

Chapter 6

CANCRO, R. "Increased Diagnostic Reliability in Schizophrenia: Some Values and Limitations." *International Journal of Psychiatry*, 1973, *11*, 53–57.

The author describes his view of the problems of diagnostic reliability in schizophrenia. He proposes a system that attempts to deal with the geographic differences in diagnostic habits.

FEIGHNER, A., AND OTHERS. "Diagnostic Criteria for Use in Psychiatric Research." *Archives of General Psychiatry,* 1972, *26,* 57–63.

This paper, which analyzes the literature, contains an excellent proposal for psychiatric research. Feighner proposes, much as we do, that schizophrenia is a chronic illness and that the diagnosis must be reserved for individuals who have chronic disabilities. These rigid criteria for including someone in the diagnostic category of schizophrenia are meant for use in research so that populations can be compared from one study to another. However, the criteria are of less value in clinical application.

MENDEL, W. "Precision in the Diagnosis of Schizophrenia." *Psychiatria Fennica,* 1975, 107–114.

In this article we describe changes in diagnosis over twenty-five years in a series of 470 cases of schizophrenia. The diagnosis of schizoaffective schizophrenia is totally unstable. The diagnosis of acute schizophrenia seems to suit an illness entirely different from chronic schizophrenia.

STRAUSS, J., AND CARPENTER, W. "Characteristic Symptoms and Outcome in Schizophrenia." *American Journal of Psychiatry,* 1974, *30,* 429–434.

Here is an attempt to relate diagnostic criteria to the outcome of the illness. Many useful attempts have been made along this line. The authors seem to imply that the diagnosis of schizophrenia really must be reserved for those cases in which a long-term history is available.

WINOKUR, G. "Diagnostic Stability Over Time in Schizophrenia, Mania and Depression." *New England Journal of Medicine,* 1974, *290,* 1026–1032.

In this article Winokur attempts to study the diagnostic stability of mania, depression, and schizophrenia. This author found that the diagnostic category of schizoaffective schizophrenia resolved itself either into schizophrenia or into mania after several years of follow-up study.

Chapter 7

BLEULER, M. "A 23-Year Longitudinal Study of 208 Schizophrenics and Impressions in Regard to the Nature of Schizophrenia." In D.

Rosenthal and S. S. Kety (Eds.), *The Transmission of Schizophrenia*. Oxford: Pergamon Press, 1968.

Manfred Bleuler is the son of Eugen Bleuler, who originated the term *schizophrenia*. Here M. Bleuler followed twenty-eight patients in a longitudinal study. He describes his impressions of the nature of schizophrenia and comes to the conclusion that the primary and major difficulty is the autism. Therefore, according to M. Bleuler, ambivalence, loosening of associations, and affective inappropriateness and flatness are no longer essential to the diagnosis; only autism remains.

FOWLER, R., AND OTHERS. "The Validity of Good Prognosis Schizophrenia." *Archives of General Psychiatry*, 1972, *26*, 182–185.

The authors discuss the differences between good-prognosis and poor-prognosis schizophrenia, a problem that has occupied researchers in the literature for the past fifty years. However, these authors, like others, look for prognosis in the type of schizophrenia and in the course of illness. We predict outcome not on the basis of schizophrenia but on the basis of all other aspects of the patient. It seems to us that what the patient has *besides* schizophrenia is what determines the outcome.

STRAUSS, J., AND CARPENTER, W. "The Prediction of Outcome in Schizophrenia." *Archives of General Psychiatry*, 1974, *31*, 37–42.

This contribution is another recent attempt at predicting outcome. These authors in a series of articles have made the best and most serious attempt at outcome study in recent times. At present there are two major approaches to prediction of outcome. One is to attempt to predict outcome on the basis of premorbid personality and type of onset. The other is to predict outcome on the basis of the course of the illness itself. We reject both of these approaches and maintain that the best prediction of outcome is a focus on the assets a patient has in his personality, talents, and adaptive capacity with which he manages his life with schizophrenia.

Chapter 8

HESTON, L. "Psychiatric Disorders in Foster Home Reared Children in Schizophrenic Mothers." *British Journal of Psychiatry*, 1966, *112*, 819–825.

A survey of genetic evidence through 1972 by the individual who carried out the first adopted-away offspring study. On the whole, a rather balanced and concise summary of far-ranging genetic material. It also summarizes his notion of a genetic "schizoid spectrum," a controversial concept that lumps together a variety of nonschizophrenic conditions as genetically linked to the fully manifested disease.

KARLSSON, J. "A Two-Locus Hypothesis for Inheritance of Schizo-phrenia." In A. R. Kaplan (Ed.), *Genetic Factors in Schizo-phrenia.* Springfield, Ill.: Charles C. Thomas, 1972.

An example of a type of genetic article offering a hypothesis for the type of genetic transmission occurring in schizo-phrenia. It should be pointed out that no structural genetic hypothesis has been proven and available fact can fit into several different ones. The book in which the article appears is a rather haphazard assortment of a variety of articles on genetics that would be of interest to anyone wishing to pursue the evidence further. It probably includes more than anyone would want to know about genes and schizophrenia.

KETY, S., AND OTHERS. "Mental Illness in the Biological and Adoptive Families of Adopted Individuals Who Have Become Schizo-phrenic: A Preliminary Report Based Upon Psychiatric Interviews." In R. Fieve, H. Brill, and D. Rosenthal (Eds.), *Genetics and Psychopathology.* Baltimore: Johns Hopkins Press, in press.

The probably final and certainly to this date definitive study of adopted-away offspring and schizophrenia. A masterful work of research that seems to lay aside all arguments about previous studies of adopted-away individuals.

SHIELDS, J. "Summary of the Genetic Evidence." In D. Rosenthal and S. Kety (Eds.), *The Transmission of Schizophrenia.* Oxford: Pergamon Press, 1968.

At its time, this article was the best summary of the evidence indicating genetic factors in schizophrenia. Still a classic article, it is particularly good in its evaluation of the accuracy of cited studies. The volume of which it is a part is also an excellent source for surveys of any theories connected with the transmission of schizophrenia, not only those theories based on genetics but also on communications, socioeconomics, and so on. Though the work is nearly ten years old, it remains a very useful basic reference.

Chapter 9

FROHMAN, C. "Plasma Proteins and Schizophrenia." In J. Mendels (Ed.), *Biological Psychiatry*. New York: John Wiley & Sons, 1973.

An excellent review of the literature on plasma proteins in schizophrenia with heavy emphasis on his own work and the work of the LaFayette Clinic. A good example of the vagaries and vicissitudes of research in the biochemical aspects of schizophrenia.

SNYDER, S. "Catecholamines in the Brain as Mediators of Amphetamine Psychosis." *Archives of General Psychiatry*, 1972, *27*, 169–179.

The most lucid and forceful proponent of the dopamine-amphetamine hypothesis of schizophrenia. The hypothesis has many attractive features both clinically and psychopharmacologically. Although presently the front runner, the theory is by no means proven at this time.

STEIN, L., AND WISE, C. "Possible Etiology of Schizophrenia: Progressive Damage to the Noradrenergic Reward System by B-Hydroxydopamine." *Science*, 1973, *181*, 344–347.

This article presents another catecholamine hypothesis for the basic deficits in schizophrenia. The hypothesis is especially interesting in light of the fact that it explains the difference between acute and chronic schizophrenia. Although many people have jumped on the amphetamine bandwagon, few people tend to be involved with the B-hydroxydopamine theory of Stein and Wise, even though it is perhaps philosophically more interesting than the amphetamine theory.

Chapter 10

BATESON, G. "Minimal Requirements for a Theory of Schizophrenia." *Archives of General Psychiatry*, 1960, *2*, 477–491.

Bateson proposes the theory that the etiology of schizophrenia is related to the double-bind situation in which children who receive conflicting signals from the significant adults find themselves unable to act. Although there is no evidence to support this theory as a basis for understanding the etiology of schizophrenia, it is clearly observable that, in adult schizophrenic patients, ambiguous signals and confusing double-bind situations cause exacerbation of symptoms. Therefore, techniques of treatment must result in clear and simple instructions to the patient in which the verbal and nonverbal content of the psychotherapeutic transaction conveys the same message.

JACKSON, E. (Ed.), *The Etiology of Schizophrenia*. New York: Basic Books, 1959.

The author reviews various theories of etiology of schizophrenia in this 1960 edition. This book is an excellent summary of various nonbiological theories of schizophrenia proposed before 1960.

LEE, I. *Language Habits in Human Affairs*. New York: Harper & Bros., 1941.

This book suggests the germ of the idea that how we use language is a reflection of how we think and that how we think may be closely related to the kinds of difficulties in living that people experience. This idea has been enlarged by some theoreticians to the generalization that schizophrenia is entirely the result of the difficulty in thinking and language found in such patients.

SULLIVAN, H. *Schizophrenia as a Human Process*. New York: W. W. Norton, 1962.

In this book, Sullivan proposes his interpersonal relationships theory as the basis for understanding schizophrenia. He sees all of the major difficulties of the schizophrenic patient as being secondary to the impairment of self-esteem. We feel, however, that the impairment of self-esteem is in fact secondary to the three clusters of disabilities that we have described in some detail in our present book.

Chapter 11

KETY, S. "From Rationalization to Reason." *American Journal of Psychiatry*, 1974, *131*, 957–963.

In this paper Kety, who is one of the leading summarizers of biochemical and genetic theories of schizophrenia, reviews the state of the art in the year 1974.

LEWIS, A. "Manfred Bleuler's 'The Schizophrenia Mental Disorders: An Exposition and a Review.'" *Psychological Medicine*, 1973, *3*, 385–392.

The author reviews Bleuler's ideas about the etiology of schizophrenia and compares them to other ideas presented in the literature.

SELYE, H. *The Story of the Adaptation Syndrome.* Montreal: Acta, 1952.

The famous physician outlines his theory of illness in terms of the diseases of adaptation. Adaptive responses, when they have become maladaptive, become diseases of adaptation. Precisely the same model is used in psychiatry within the neo-Freudian system of psychopathology, in which normal defense (coping) mechanisms become neuroses at that point when they become maladaptive rather than adaptive. The psychoanalytic model of neuroses is thus within the model of diseases of adaptation. Some people feel that schizophrenia too is a disease or syndrome of adaptation in which adaptive responses to internal and external stress have become maladaptive and become the basis of the syndrome.

Chapter 12

HALEY, J. *Strategies of Psychotherapy.* New York: Grune & Stratton, 1963.

The author offers detailed discussion of ways of using interpersonal transactions as a basis of providing the corrective emotional experience for psychological illness. There are many authors who have proposed that corrective emotional experience can be of help to the schizophrenic patient. However, the difficulty is that even though therapy based on an interpersonal relationship is the backbone of any treatment of schizophrenia, the patients, because of their psychopathology, usually manage to have the psychotherapeutic relationship come out as badly as they have managed other relationships in life. Therefore, treatment takes special skills and a very special understanding on the part of the therapist.

MAY, P. *Treatment of Schizophrenia.* New York: Science House, 1968.

This book presents a comparison of treatment of schizophrenia by psychotherapy with medications, psychotherapy without medication, and electroconvulsive therapy. The results of electroconvulsive therapy and of medication are approximately the same as, and vastly superior to, psychotherapy by itself.

SIIRALA, M. "Psychotherapy of Schizophrenia as Basic Human Experience." *Psychiatria Fennica,* 1972, 155–175.

    In this fine article, the treatment of schizophrenia is seen
as an interpersonal transaction closely resembling the corrective
emotional experience of reparenting.

Chapter 13

CAPLAN, G. *Theory and Practice of Mental Health Consultation.* New
York: Basic Books, 1970.

    This contribution has become the basic article in the
theory of crisis intervention. Much has been written since 1965
on this subject, but all of the material is essentially an elaboration of the point of view first presented by Caplan.

VONNEGUT, M. "Why I Want to Bite R. D. Laing." *Harper's,* April
1974, *248,* 90–93.

    This brief article, written by a patient later turned
physician, seriously indicts the philosophical nondisease approach to schizophrenia. Subsequent to this article, the author
wrote *The Eden Express,* detailing his experiences with mental
illness.

Chapter 14

ODENHEIMER, J. "Day Hospital as an Alternative to the Psychiatric
Ward." *Archives of General Psychiatry,* 1965, *13,* 13–46.

    This article describes the technique of using alternatives
to psychiatric hospitalization in the care of the chronic patient.
Much has been written about this subject in the past few years
and it has become apparent that the hospitalization of patients
frequently is the result of repetitive patterns of professional
practice rather than a response to the needs of the patients.

PASAMANICK, B., SCARPITTI, F., AND DINITZ, S. *Schizophrenics in the
Community.* New York: Appleton-Century-Crofts, 1967.

    In this excellent book the authors describe the treatment
of chronic schizophrenic patients in the community and compare
the results to those obtained by treating patients in hospitals. It
is the beginning of a long-term study that hoped to assess cost to
patients, families, and communities of maintaining individuals
who live schizophrenic lives in the community rather than in

the hospital. Unfortunately, the five- and ten-year follow-up was not adequately completed because of changes in funding and policy for this study.

Chapter 15

BLEULER, M. "The Long-term Course of the Schizophrenic Psychoses." *Psychological Medicine*, 1974, *4*, 244–254.

In this article Manfred Bleuler reviews his observation, over some twenty-five to thirty years, of cases diagnosed as having schizophrenia.

SCHWING, G. *A Way to the Soul of the Mentally Ill.* New York: International Universities Press, 1954.

In this classic, a gifted author describes her approach to the long-term treatment of schizophrenia, giving anecdotal material of a case.

SECHEHAYE, M. *Reality Lost and Regained. Autobiography of a Schizophrenic Girl.* New York: Grune & Stratton, 1951.

Detailed subjective descriptions of the patient suffering from a schizophrenic illness, such as the one given here, are of great value to all therapists dealing with such patients. An understanding of the patient's feelings will lead to a clearer recognition of the meaning of symptoms and of the requirements for therapy.

Bibliography

This bibliography combines references for intext citations as well as other sources drawn on by the author of this book.

ALEXANDER, F., EISENSTEIN, S., AND GROTJAHN, M. *Psychoanalytic Pioneers*. New York: Basic Books, 1966.

ARIETI, S. *Interpretation of Schizophrenia*. New York: Brunner/Mazel, 1955.

BAKWIN, H., AND BAKWIN, R. M. *Behavior Disorders in Children* (4th ed.). Saunders, 1972.

BAN, T. A. *Recent Advances in the Biology of Schizophrenia*. Springfield, Ill.: Charles C. Thomas, 1973.

155

BANNISTER, D. "The Logical Requirement of Research into Schizophrenia." *British Journal of Psychiatry,* 1968, *114,* 181–188.

BASIT, A. "An Investigation of Leonhard's Classification of Chronic Schizophrenia." *Psychiatric Quarterly,* 1971, *45,* 172–181.

BATESON, G. "Minimal Requirements for a Theory of Schizophrenia." *Archives of General Psychiatry,* 1960, *2,* 477–491.

BAUMEYER, F. "The Schreber Case." *International Journal of Psychoanalysis,* 1956, *37,* 61–74.

BERLYNE, D. E. *Structure and Direction in Thinking.* New York: John Wiley & Sons, 1965.

BESSELL, H., AND MAZZANTI, V. "Diagnosis of Ambulatory Schizophrenia: A Case Study." *Psychiatric Quarterly,* 1959, *33,* 429–436.

BINSWANGER, L. "Symptom und Zeit." *Schweizerische Medizinische Wochenschrift,* 1951, *81,* 510–512.

BINSWANGER, L. "The Case of Ellen West." In R. May, E. Angel, and H. Ellenberger (Eds.), *Existence.* New York: Basic Books, 1958.

BINSWANGER, L. "Existential Analysis, Psychiatry, Schizophrenia." *Journal of Existential Psychiatry,* 1960, *2,* 157–165.

BLASHFIELD, R. "An Evaluation of the DMS-II Classification of Schizophrenia as a Nomenclature." *Journal of Abnormal Psychology,* 1973, *82,* 382–389.

BLEULER, E. *Dementia Praecox, or the Group of Schizophrenias.* New York: International Universities Press, 1950.

BLEULER, M. "Conception of Schizophrenia Within the Last Fifty Years and Today." *International Journal of Psychiatry,* 1965, *1,* 500–523.

BLEULER, M. "A 23-Year Longitudinal Study of 208 Schizophrenics and Impressions in Regard to the Nature of Schizophrenia." In D. Rosenthal and S. S. Kety (Eds.), *The Transmission of Schizophrenia.* Oxford: Pergamon Press, 1968.

BLEULER, M. "Some Results of Research in Schizophrenia." *Behavioral Science,* 1970, *15,* 211–219.

BLEULER, M. "Today's Concept of Schizophrenia." *Transactions & Studies of the College of Physicians of Philadelphia,* 1973, *41,* 69–80.

BLEULER, M. "The Long-Term Course of the Schizophrenic Psychoses." *Psychological Medicine,* 1974, *4,* 244–254.

BLINDER, M. "Schizophrenia: A Proposal for Nomenclature." *American Journal of Psychiatry,* 1974, *131,* 609.

BOYER, L., AND GIOVANCCHINI, P. "Office Treatment of Schizophrenic Patients: The Use of Psychoanalytic Therapy with Few

Parameters." In L. Boyer and P. Giovancchini (Eds.), *Psychoanalytic Treatment of Characterological and Schizophrenic Disorders.* New York: Science House, 1967.

BRODY, E., AND REDLICH, F. (Eds.) *Psychotherapy with Schizophrenics.* New York: International Universities Press, 1952.

BROMET, E., AND HARROW, M. "Behavioral Overinclusion as a Prognostic Index in Schizophrenic Disorders." *Journal of Abnormal Psychology,* 1973, *82,* 345–349.

BROWN, N. *Life Against Death.* New York: Vintage Books, 1959.

BURTON, A., LOPEZ-IBOR, J., AND MENDEL, W. *Schizophrenia as a Life Style.* New York: Springer, 1974.

CAMERON, M. "Introjection, Reprojection, and Hallucination in the Interaction Between Schizophrenic Patient and the Therapist." *International Journal of Psychiatry,* 1961, *42,* 86–96.

CANCRO, R. "Increased Diagnostic Reliability in Schizophrenia: Some Values and Limitations." *International Journal of Psychiatry,* 1973, *11,* 53–57.

CAPLAN, G. *Theory and Practice of Mental Health Consultation.* New York: Basic Books, 1970.

CARPENTER, W., STRAUSS, J., AND MULEH, S. "Are There Pathognomonic Symptoms in Schizophrenia?" *Archives of General Psychiatry,* 1973, *28,* 847–852.

CARTER, M., AND WATTS, C. "Possible Biological Advantages among Schizophrenics' Relatives." *British Journal of Psychiatry,* 1971, *118,* 453–460.

CHODOFF, P. "Late Effects of the Concentration Camp Syndrome." *Archives of General Psychiatry,* 1963, *8,* 323–333.

CHODOFF, P. "The German Concentration Camp as a Psychological Stress." *Archives of General Psychiatry,* 1970, *22,* 78–87.

COHEN, R. "The Hospital as a Therapeutic Instrument." *Psychiatry,* 1958, *21,* 29–35.

COOPER, H. "Problems in Application of the Basic Criteria of Schizophrenia." *American Journal of Psychiatry,* 1960, *117,* 66–71.

COPE, O. *Man, Mind and Medicine.* Philadelphia: J. B. Lippincott, 1968.

CROUGHAN, J., WELNER, A., AND ROBINS, E. "The Group of Schizoaffective and Related Psychoses—Critique, Record, Follow-Up, and Family Studies. II. Record Studies." *Archives of General Psychiatry,* 1974, *31,* 632–637.

DAVIDSON, H. "Psychiatry and the Euphemistic Delusion." *American Journal of Psychiatry,* 1953, *110,* 310–312.

DEUTSCH, A. *The Mentally Ill in America.* New York: Columbia University Press, 1946.

DEUTSCH, H. "Some Forms of Emotional Disturbance and Their Relationship to Schizophrenia." *Psychoanalytic Quarterly,* 1942, *11,* 301–321.

DE LA GARZA, C., AND WORCHEL, P. "Time and Space Orientation in Schizophrenia." *Journal of Abnormal and Social Psychology,* 1956, *52,* 191–194.

Diagnostic and Statistical Manual of Mental Disorders (DSM-II) (2nd ed.) Washington, D.C.: American Psychiatric Association, 1968.

DOLLARD, J., AND MILLER, N. *Personality and Psychotherapy: An Analysis in Terms of Learning, Thinking and Culture.* New York: McGraw-Hill, 1950.

DOUST, J. "Studies on the Physiology of Awareness: Consciousness of the Duration of Time in Psychiatric Patients." *Diseases of the Nervous System,* 1955, *16,* 363–365.

EDWARDS, G. "Diagnosis of Schizophrenia: An Anglo-American Comparison." *British Journal of Psychiatry,* 1972, *120,* 385–390.

EISENSTEIN, V. "Differential Psychotherapy of Borderline States." *Psychiatric Quarterly,* 1951, *25,* 375–401.

EKSTEIN, R. *The Challenge: Despair and Hope in the Conquest of Inner Space.* New York: Brunner/Mazel, 1971.

ERIKSON, E. *Childhood and Society.* New York: W. W. Norton, 1950.

FAIRBAIRN, W. "Considerations Arising Out of the Schreber Case." *British Journal of Medical Psychology,* 1958, *29,* 113–117.

FALEK, A., AND MOSER, H. "Classification in Schizophrenia." *Archives of General Psychiatry,* 1975, *32,* 59–67.

FEIGHNER, A., AND OTHERS. "Diagnostic Criteria for Use in Psychiatric Research." *Archives of General Psychiatry,* 1972, *26,* 57–63.

FINK, M. "The Electroencephalogram in Clinical Psychiatry." In J. Mendels (Ed.), *Biological Psychiatry.* New York: John Wiley & Sons, 1973.

FLECK, S., AND OTHERS. "Interaction Between Hospital Staff and Families." *Psychiatry,* 1957, *20,* 343–350.

FOUCAULT, M. *Madness and Civilization.* New York: Pantheon Books, 1965.

FOWLER, R., AND OTHERS. "The Validity of Good Prognosis Schizophrenia." *Archives of General Psychiatry,* 1972, *26,* 182–185.

FRAISSE, P. *The Psychology of Time.* New York: Harper & Row, 1963.

FRANK, J. *Persuasion and Healing.* Baltimore: Johns Hopkins Press, 1961.

FRANK, J. "The Role of Hope in Psychotherapy." *International Journal of Psychiatry,* 1968, *5,* 383–400.

FREEDMAN, D. "Psychotomimetic Agents and Our Understanding of Psychiatric Disorders." In J. Mendels (Ed.), *Biological Psychiatry.* New York: John Wiley & Sons, 1973.

FREUD, A. *The Ego and the Mechanisms of Defense.* New York: International Universities Press, 1946.

FRIEDHOFF, A. "Biogenic Amines and Schizophrenia." In J. Mendels (Ed.), *Biological Psychiatry.* New York: John Wiley & Sons, 1973.

FRIEDMAN, H. "Perceptual Regression in Schizophrenia: A Hypothesis Suggested by the Rorschach Test." *Journal of Genetic Psychology,* 1952, *81,* 63–98.

FROHMAN, C. "Plasma Proteins and Schizophrenia." In J. Mendels (Ed.), *Biological Psychiatry.* New York: John Wiley & Sons, 1973.

FROMM-REICHMAN, F. "Transference Problems in Schizophrenia." *Psychoanalytic Quarterly,* 1939, *8,* 412–426.

FROMM-REICHMAN, F. *Principles of Intensive Psychotherapy.* Chicago: University of Chicago Press, 1950.

GELLHORN, E., AND KIELY, W. "Autonomic Nervous System in Psychiatric Disorder." In J. Mendels (Ed.), *Biological Psychiatry.* New York: John Wiley & Sons, 1973.

GIOVACCHINI, P. "A Reappraisal of the Dementia Praecox Concept—In Elaboration." *International Journal of Psychiatry,* 1972, *10,* 41–44.

GOODWIN, D., ALDERSON, P., AND ROSENTHAL, R. "Clinical Significance of Hallucinations in Psychiatric Disorders." *Archives of General Psychiatry,* 1971, *24,* 76–80.

GREEN, G. "Studies in the Psychopathology of Time: I. An Exploration of Temporal Behavior in Schizophrenia." *Unpublished doctoral dissertation,* University of Southern California, 1963.

GUNDERSON, J., AND SINGER, M. "Defining Borderline Patients: An Overview." *American Journal of Psychiatry,* 1975, *132,* 1–10.

GUNDERSON, AND OTHERS. "Schizophrenia, 1974." Washington, D.C.: *Schizophrenia Bulletin,* 1974, *9,* 16–54.

HALEY, J. *Strategies of Psychotherapy.* New York: Grune & Stratton, 1963.

HARLEY-MASON, R. "Appendix." In Osmond, H., and Smythies, J. "Schizophrenia. A New Approach." *Journal of Mental Science,* 1952, *98,* 309–315.

HARLOW, H., AND ZIMMERMAN, R. "Affectional Responses in the Infant Monkey." *Science,* 1959, *130,* 421–432.

HEATH, R., AND OTHERS. "Behavioral Changes in Nonpsychotic Volunteers Following the Administration of Taraxein, the Substance Obtained From Serum of Schizophrenic Patients." *American Journal of Psychiatry,* 1958, *114,* 917–920.

HEIDEGGER, M. "Sein und Zeit." *Jahrbuch für Philosophie und Phenomenologische Forschung,* 1927, *8,* 1–438.

HESTON, L. "Psychiatric Disorders in Foster Home Reared Children in Schizophrenic Mothers." *British Journal of Psychiatry,* 1966, *112,* 819–825.

HESTON, L. "Genes and Schizophrenia." In J. Mendels (Ed.), *Biological Psychiatry.* New York: John Wiley & Sons, 1973.

HOCH, P., AND POLATIN, P. "Pseudoneurotic Forms of Schizophrenia." *Psychiatric Quarterly,* 1949, *23,* 248–276.

INGUAR, D., AND FRANZEN, G. "Abnormalities of Cerebral Blood Flow Distribution in Patients with Chronic Schizophrenia." *Acta Psychiatrica Scandinavica,* 1974, *50,* 425–462.

The International Pilot Study of Schizophrenia. Geneva: World Health Organization, 1973.

JACKSON, D. (Ed.) *The Etiology of Schizophrenia.* New York: Basic Books, 1959.

JAHODA, M. *Current Concepts of Positive Mental Health.* New York: Basic Books, 1959.

JASPERS, K. *General Psychopathology.* (J. Hoenig and M. Hamilton, Trans.) Chicago: University of Chicago Press, 1963.

KALLMANN, F. *The Genetics of Schizophrenia.* New York: J. Augustin, 1938.

KALLMANN, F. "The Genetic Theory of Schizophrenia: An Analysis of 691 Schizophrenic Twin Index Families." *American Journal of Psychiatry,* 1946, *103,* 309–322.

KANT, I. *The Classification of Mental Disorders.* (Charles T. Sullivan, Trans.) Doylestown, Pa.: The Doylestown Foundation, 1964. (Originally published in German in 1798.)

KARDINER, A., KARUSH, A., AND OVESEY, L. "A Methodological Study of Freudian Theory." *International Journal of Psychiatry,* 1966, *2,* 489–596.

KARLSSON, J. "A Two-Locus Hypothesis for Inheritance of Schizophrenia." In A. R. Kaplan (Ed.), *Genetic Factors in Schizo-phrenia*. Springfield, Ill.: Charles C. Thomas, 1972.

KARON, B., AND VANDENBOS, G. "Experience, Medication, and the Effectiveness of Psychotherapy with Schizophrenics." *British Journal of Psychiatry*, 1970, *116*, 427–428.

KENDELL, R., AND GOURLAY, J. "The Clinical Distinction Between the Affective Psychoses and Schizophrenia." *British Journal of Psychiatry*, 1970, *117*, 261–266.

KERNBERG, O. "Borderline Personality Organization." *Journal of the American Psychoanalytic Association*, 1967, *15*, 641–685.

KETY, S. "Biochemical Theories of Schizophrenia," I, II. *Science*, 1959, *129*, 1528–1532 and 1590–1596.

KETY, S. "Prospects for Research in Schizophrenia—An Overview." *Neuroscience Research Progress Bulletin*, 1972, *10*, 456–467.

KETY, S. "Problems in Biological Research in Psychiatry." In J. Mendels (Ed.), *Biological Psychiatry*. New York: John Wiley & Sons, 1973.

KETY, S. "From Rationalization to Reason." *American Journal of Psychiatry*, 1974, *131*, 957–963.

KETY, S., AND OTHERS. "Mental Illness in the Biological and Adoptive Families of Adopted Individuals Who Have Become Schizo-phrenic: A Preliminary Report Based Upon Psychiatric Inter-views. In R. Fieve, H. Brill, and D. Rosenthal (Eds.), *Genetics and Psychopathology*. Baltimore: Johns Hopkins Press, 1976.

KIND, H. "The Psychogenesis of Schizophrenia." *International Journal of Psychiatry*, 1967, *3*, 383–417.

KLEIN, M. *Narrative of Child Analysis*. New York: Basic Books, 1961.

KNIGHT, R. "Borderline States." *Bulletin of the Menninger Clinic*, 1953, *17*, 1–12.

KRAEPELIN, E. *Lectures on Clinical Psychiatry*. New York: William Wood, 1904.

KRIS, A. "A Reappraisal of the Dementia Praecox Concept. II. Case Studies in Chronic Hospitalization for Functional Psychosis." *International Journal of Psychiatry*, 1972, *10*, 18–40.

KURIANSKY, J., DEMING, W., AND GURLAND, B. "On Trends in the Diagnosis of Schizophrenia." *American Journal of Psychiatry*, 1974, *131*, 402–408.

LAING, R. *The Divided Self*. London: Pelican, 1965.

LANGSLEY, D. *The Treatment of Families in Crisis*. New York: Grune & Stratton, 1968.

LANZKRON, J., AND WOLFSON, W. "Prognostic Value of Perceptual

Distortion of Temporal Disorientation in Chronic Schizophrenia." *American Journal of Psychiatry,* 1958, *114,* 744–746.

LASSENIUS, B., OTTOSSON, J., AND RAPP, W. "Prognosis in Schizophrenia. The Need for Institutionalized Care." *Acta Psychiatrica Scandinavica,* 1973, *49,* 295–305.

LEE, I. *Language Habits in Human Affairs.* New York: Harper & Bros., 1941.

LEENDERT, B., AND GRUNBAUM, A. "Eine Störung der Chronologie und ihre Bedeutung im Betreffenden Symptomenbild." *Monatsschrift für Psychiatrie und Neurologie,* 1929, *73,* 1–39.

LEHMANN, H. "Pharmacotherapy in Schizophrenia." In J. Zubin (Ed.), *Psychopathology of Schizophrenia.* New York: Grune & Stratton, 1966.

LEUNER, H. *Die Experimentelle Psychose.* Berlin: Springer, 1962.

LEWIS, A. "Manfred Bleuler's 'The Schizophrenia Mental Disorders: An Exposition and a Review.'" *Psychological Medicine,* 1973, *3,* 385–392.

LEWIS, N. *The Constitutional Factors in Dementia Praecox.* Monograph Series No. 35. New York: Nervous and Mental Disease, 1923.

LOWE, G. "The Phenomenology of Hallucinations as an Aid to Differential Diagnosis." *British Journal of Psychiatry,* 1973, *123,* 621–633.

LUFT, R. "Some Considerations on the Pathogenesis of Diabetes Mellitus." *New England Journal of Medicine,* 1968, *279,* 1086–1092.

MAHLER, M., AND ELKISCH, P. "Some Observations on Disturbances of the Ego in a Case of Infantile Psychosis." *Psychoanalytic Study of the Child,* 1953, *8,* 252–261.

MALZBERG, B. "Age and Sex in Relation to Mental Diseases." *Mental Hygiene,* 1955, *39,* 196–224.

MAY, P. *Treatment of Schizophrenia.* New York: Science House, 1968.

MAZZANTI, V., AND BESSELL, H. "Communication Through Latent Language." *American Journal of Psychotherapy,* 1956, *10,* 250–260.

MEDNICK, S. "Breakdown in Individuals at High Risk for Schizophrenia: Possible Predispositional Perinatal Factors." *Mental Hygiene,* 1970, *54,* 50–63.

MELLOR, C. "First Rank Symptoms of Schizophrenia." *British Journal of Psychiatry,* 1970, *117,* 15–23.

MELLSOP, G., SPELMAN, M., AND HARRISON, A. "Thought Disorder in Manics and Schizophrenics." *British Journal of Psychiatry,* 1972, *121,* 454.

MENDEL, E. *Text-Book of Psychiatry.* (W. C. Krauss, Trans.) Philadelphia: F. A. Davis, 1907.

MENDEL, W. "Expansion of a Shrunken World." *The Journal of the Association for Physical and Mental Rehabilitation,* 1959, *1,* 5–9.

MENDEL, W. "The Future in the Model of Psychopathology." *Journal of Existential Psychiatry,* 1962, *2,* 363–370.

MENDEL, W. "Existential Emphasis in Psychiatry." *American Journal of Psychoanalysis,* 1963, *23,* 1–4.

MENDEL, W. "The Medical Interview." *General Practice,* 1964a, *29,* 118–124.

MENDEL, W. "Outpatient Therapy of Chronic Schizophrenia." In J. Masserman (Ed.), *Current Psychiatric Therapies.* Vol. 4. New York: Grune & Stratton, 1964b.

MENDEL, W. "The Phenomenon of Interpretation." *American Journal of Psychoanalysis,* 1964c, *24,* 184–189.

MENDEL, W. "The Anxious Patient." *California Medicine,* 1965, *102,* 123–126.

MENDEL, W. "Effect of Length of Hospitalization on Rate and Quality of Remission From Acute Psychotic Episodes." *Journal of Nervous and Mental Disease,* 1966a, *143,* 226–233.

MENDEL, W. "Problems of Human Identity." *Existential Psychiatry,* 1966b, *1,* 220–223.

MENDEL, W. "Tranquilizer Prescribing as a Function of the Experience and Availability of the Therapist." *American Journal of Psychiatry,* 1967, *124,* 16–22.

MENDEL, W. "The Non-Specifics of Psychotherapy." *International Journal of Psychiatry,* 1968a, *5,* 400–402.

MENDEL, W. "On the Abolition of the Psychiatric Hospital." In L. Roberts, and others (Eds.), *Comprehensive Mental Health.* Madison: University of Wisconsin Press, 1968b.

MENDEL, W. "Responsibility in Health, Illness, and Treatment." *Archives of General Psychiatry,* 1968c, *18,* 697–705.

MENDEL, W. "Authority: Its Nature and Use in the Therapeutic Relationship." *Hospital and Community Psychiatry,* 1970, *21,* 367–370.

MENDEL, W. "Depression and Suicide—Treatment and Prevention." *Consultant,* 1972, *12,* 115–116.

MENDEL, W. "Precision in the Diagnosis of Schizophrenia." *Psychiatria Fennica,* 1975a, 107–114.

MENDEL, W. *Supportive Care: Theory and Technique.* Los Angeles: Mara Books, 1975b.

MENDEL, W., AND GREEN, G. *The Therapeutic Management of Psychological Illness.* New York: Basic Books, 1967.

MENDEL, W., AND RAPPORT, S. "Outpatient Treatment for Chronic Schizophrenic Patients." *Archives of General Psychiatry,* 1963, *8,* 190–196.

MENDEL, W., AND RAPPORT, S. "Determinants of the Decision for Psychiatric Hospitalization." *Archives of General Psychiatry,* 1969, *20,* 320–328.

MENDEL, W., AND WEXLER, M. "Perceptual Organization of Schizophrenic Patients." *Existential Psychiatry,* 1967, *6,* 145–153.

MENNINGER, K. *A Manual for Psychiatric Case Study.* New York: Grune & Stratton, 1952.

MERSKEY, H. "Diagnosis of Schizophrenia." *Lancet,* 1972, *2,* 1246–1249.

MEYER, A. "The Nature and Conception of Dementia Praecox." *The Journal of Abnormal Psychology,* 1910, *5,* 274–285.

MINKOWSKI, E. *Le Temps vécu.* Paris: Collection de l'Evolution Psychiatrique, 1933.

MISHLER, E., AND SCOTCH, N. "Sociocultural Factors in the Epidemiology of Schizophrenia." *International Journal of Psychiatry,* 1965, *1,* 258–305.

MISHLER, E., AND WAXLER, N. "Family Interaction Processes and Schizophrenia: A Review of Current Theories." *International Journal of Psychiatry,* 1966, *2,* 375–430.

MORRISON, J., AND OTHERS. "The Iowa 500. I. Diagnostic Validity in Mania, Depression and Schizophrenia." *Archives of General Psychiatry,* 1972, *27,* 457–461.

MYERS, J., AND ROBERTS, B. *Family and Class Dynamics.* New York: John Wiley & Sons, 1959.

NAGERA, H. *Vincent van Gogh: A Psychological Study.* New York: International Universities Press, 1967.

ODENHEIMER, J. "Day Hospital as an Alternative to the Psychiatric Ward." *Archives of General Psychiatry,* 1965, *13,* 13–46.

OFFER, D., AND SABSHIN, M. *Normality.* New York: Basic Books, 1966.

PARAD, H., AND CAPLAN, G. "A Framework for Studying Families in Crisis." In H. Parad (Ed.), *Crisis Intervention.* New York: Family Service Association, 1965.

PARFITT, D. "The Neurology of Schizophrenia." *Journal of Mental Science*, 1956, *102*, 671–718.

PARSONS, T. "Illness and the Role of the Physician." In C. Kluckhohn and H. A. Murray (Eds.), *Personality in Nature, Society, and Culture*. New York: Alfred A. Knopf, 1952.

PARSONS, T. "Definitions of Health and Illness in the Light of American Values and Social Structure." In E. G. Jaco (Ed.), *Patients, Physicians and Illness*. New York: Free Press, 1958.

PASAMANICK, B., SCARPITTI, F., AND DINITZ, S. *Schizophrenics in the Community*. New York: Appleton-Century-Crofts, 1967.

PAYNE, R. "Disorders of Thinking." In C. G. Costello (Ed.), *Symptoms of Psychopathology: A Handbook*. New York: John Wiley & Sons, 1970.

PENMAN, J. "Pain as an Old Friend." *Lancet*, 1954, *266*, 633–636.

POLATIN, R., AND HOCH, P. "Diagnostic Evaluation of Early Schizophrenia." *Journal of Nervous and Mental Disease*, 1947, *105*, 221–230.

POPE INNOCENT VIII. *Malleus Maleficarum*. (Rev. Montague Summers, Trans.) London: Pushkin Press, 1928.

RAMZY, I., AND WALLERSTEIN, R. "Pain, Fear and Anxiety." *The Psychoanalytic Study of the Child*, 1959, *13*, 147–189.

REID, A. "Schizophrenia—Disease or Syndrome?" *Archives of General Psychiatry*, 1973, *28*, 863–869.

ROBINS, E., AND GUZE, S. "Establishment of Diagnostic Validity in Psychiatric Illness: Its Application to Schizophrenia." *American Journal of Psychiatry*, 1970, *126*, 983–987.

ROSEN, J. *Direct Psychoanalytic Psychiatry*. New York: Grune & Stratton, 1962.

SAUL, L., AND PULVER, S. "The Concept of Emotional Maturity." *International Journal of Psychiatry*, 1967, *2*, 446–470.

SARBIN, T. "On the Futility of the Proposition that Some People Be Labeled Mentally Ill." *Journal of Consulting Psychology*, 1967, *31*, 447–453.

SCHILDER, P. "Psychopathology of Time." *Journal of Nervous and Mental Disease*, 1936, *83*, 530–546.

SCHMIDEBERG, M. "The Borderline Patient." In S. Arieti (Ed.), *American Handbook of Psychiatry, I*. New York: Basic Books, 1959.

SCHNEIDER, K. *Clinical Psychopathology*. New York: Grune & Stratton, 1959.

SCHWING, G. *A Way to the Soul of the Mentally Ill*. New York: International Universities Press, 1954.

SCOTT, W. "Some Psycho-Dynamic Aspects of Disturbed Perception Of Time." *British Journal of Medical Psychology*, 1948, *21*, 111–120.

SEARLES, H. "Transference Psychosis in the Psychotherapy of Schizophrenia." *International Journal of Psychoanalysis*, 1963, *44*, 249–281.

SEARLES, H. "The Schizophrenic Individual's Experience of His World." *Psychiatry*, 1967, *30*, 119–131.

SEBSHIN, M., AND OTHERS. "Conference on Normal Behavior." *Archives of General Psychiatry*, 1967, *17*, 258–330.

SECHEHAYE, M. *Autobiography of a Schizophrenic Girl*. New York: Grune & Stratton, 1951a.

SECHEHAYE, M. *Symbolic Realization*. New York: International Universities Press, 1951b.

SELYE, H. *The Story of the Adaptation Syndrome*. Montreal: Acta, 1952.

SHEPS, J. "Group Therapy in Schizophrenia." In L. Kolb and others (Eds.), *Schizophrenia*, International Psychiatry Clinics, Vol. 1, No. 4. Boston: Little Brown, 1964.

SHIELDS, J. "Summary of the Genetic Evidence." In D. Rosenthal and S. Kety (Eds.), *The Transmission of Schizophrenia*. Oxford: Pergamon Press, 1968.

SHIELDS, J., GOTTESMAN, I., AND SLATER, E. "Kallmann's 1946 Schizophrenic Twin Study in the Light of New Information." *Acta Psychiatrica Scandinavica*, 1967, *43*, 385–396.

SIIRALA, M. "Psychotherapy of Schizophrenia as Basic Human Experience." *Psychiatria Fennica*, 1972, 155–175.

SIMON, R., AND OTHERS. "Relationship Between Psychopathology and British- or American-Oriented Diagnosis." *Journal of Abnormal Psychology*, 1971, *78*, 26–29.

SLOANE, R., AND OTHERS. "Prognosis in Schizophrenia." Personal communication, September 1974.

SNYDER, S. "Catecholamines in the Brain as Mediators of Amphetamine Psychosis." *Archives of General Psychiatry*, 1972, *27*, 169–179.

SNYDER, S., AND OTHERS. "Drugs, Neurotransmitters and Schizophrenia." *Science*, 1974, *184*, 1243–1253.

SPITZ, R. A., AND COBLINER, W. G. *First Year of Life: A Psychoanalytic Study of Normal and Deviant Development of Object Relations*. New York: International Universities Press, 1966.

STEIN, L. "Dopamine-6-Hydroxylase Deficits in the Brains of Schizophrenic Patients." *Science*, 1973, *181*, 344–347.

STEIN, L., AND WISE, C. "Possible Etiology of Schizophrenia: Progressive Damage to the Noradrenergic Reward System by B-Hydroxydopamine." *Science,* 1971, *171,* 1032–1036.

STEPHENS, J., AND ASTRUP, C. "Prognosis in 'Process' and 'Non-Process' Schizophrenia." *American Journal of Psychiatry,* 1963, *119,* 945–953.

STRAUSS, J., AND CARPENTER, W. "The Prediction of Outcome in Schizophrenia. I. Characteristics of Outcome." *Archives of General Psychiatry,* 1972, *27,* 739–746.

STRAUSS, J., AND CARPENTER, W. "Characteristic Symptoms and Outcome in Schizophrenia." *American Journal of Psychiatry,* 1974a, *30,* 429–434.

STRAUSS, J., AND CARPENTER, W. "The Prediction of Outcome in Schizophrenia." *Archives of General Psychiatry,* 1974b, *31,* 37–42.

SULLIVAN, H. *Schizophrenia as a Human Process.* New York: W. W. Norton, 1962.

SZASZ, T. *The Myth of Mental Illness.* New York: Harper & Row, 1963.

TAUSK, V. "On the Origin of the 'Influencing Machine' in Schizophrenia." *Psychoanalytic Quarterly,* 1933, *2,* 519–56. Reprinted in R. Fliess (Ed.), *The Psychoanalytic Reader.* Vol. I. New York: International Universities Press, 1946.

TAYLOR, M. "Schneiderian First-Rank Symptoms and Clinical Prognostic Features in Schizophrenia." *Archives of General Psychiatry,* 1972, *26,* 64–67.

TIENARI, P. "Schizophrenia in Monozygotic Male Twins." In D. Rosenthal and S. Kety (Eds.), *The Transmission of Schizophrenia.* Oxford: Pergamon Press, 1968.

TONG, J., AND MURPHY, I. "A Review of Stress Reactivity Research in Relation to Psychopathology and Psychopathic Behavior Disorders." *Journal of Mental Science,* 1960, *106,* 1273–1295.

VAILLANT, G. "Prospective Prediction of Schizophrenic Remission." *Archives of General Psychiatry,* 1964, *11,* 509–518.

VONNEGUT, M. "Why I Want to Bite R. D. Laing." *Harper's,* April 1974, 90–93.

WELNER, A., CROUGHAN, J., AND ROBINS, E. "The Group of Schizoaffective and Related Psychoses—Critique, Record, Follow-Up, and Family Studies. I. Persistent Enigma." *Archives of General Psychiatry,* 1974, *31,* 628–631.

WILL, O. "Psychotherapeutics and the Schizophrenic Reaction." *Journal of Nervous and Mental Disease,* 1958, *126,* 109–140.

WINOKUR, G. "Diagnostic Stability Over Time in Schizophrenia, Mania and Depression." *New England Journal of Medicine,* 1974, *290,* 1026–1032.

WOLF, S., AND WOLFF, H. "Evidence of the Genesis of Peptic Ulcer in Man." *Journal of the American Medical Association,* 1942, *120,* 670–675.

WOLPE, J. *The Practice of Behavior Therapy.* New York: Pergamon Press, 1969.

WYNNE, L. "Communication Disorders and the Quest for Relatedness in Families of Schizophrenics." In R. Cancro (Ed.), *Annual Review of the Schizophrenic Syndrome,* 2. New York: Brunner/ Mazel, 1972.

YATES, A. "Data-Processing Levels and Thought Disorder in Schizophrenia," *Australian Journal of Psychology,* 1966, *18,* 103–117.

YUSIN, A. "Analysis of Crises Using A Stress-Motivation-Response Model." *American Journal of Psychotherapy,* 1974, *28,* 409–417.

ZILBOORG, G. *"Ambulatory Schizophrenias." Psychiatry,* 1941, *4,* 149–155.

ZUSMAN, J. "Some Explanations of the Changing Appearance of Psychotic Patients: Antecedents of the Social Breakdown Syndrome Concept." *International Journal of Psychiatry,* 1967, *3,* 216–247.

Index